W9-BGX-710
3 1611 00066 5783

RESISTANT INTERACTIONS

RESISTANT INTERACTIONS

Child, Family and Psychotherapist

Robert J. Marshall, Ph.D.
Private Practice
Croton-on-Hudson, NY
and New York, NY

Published by Human Sciences Press, Inc.
72 Fifth Avenue, New York, New York 10011

Printed in the United States of America
23456789 987654321

Library of Congress Cataloging in Publication Data

Marshall, Robert J., Ph. D.
Resistant interactions.

Includes index
1. Resistance (Psychoanalysis) 2. Psychotherapist and patient. 3. Mentally ill—Family relationships. I. Title
RC489.R49M28 618.92'8917 LC 82-947
ISBN 0-89885-116-5 AACR2

CONTENTS

PREFACE

> "The theory of psychoanalysis is an attempt to account for the facts of transference and resistance. Any line of investigation which recognizes these two facts and takes them as the starting point of its work has a right to call itself psychoanalysis."

Freud (1914), *On the History of the Psychoanalytic Movement*

> The intention of psycho-analysis is "to strengthen the ego, to make it more independent of the superego, to widen its field of perception and enlarge its organization, so that it can appropriate fresh portions of the id. Where id was, there ego shall be."

Freud (1933[1932]), *New Introductory Lectures to Psychoanalysis*

> "In the child's interest, it is true, analytic influences must be combined with educational measures."

Freud (1926), *The Question of Lay Analysis*

"It is often necessary to combine with a child's analysis a certain amount of analytic influencing of his parents."

Freud (1933[1932]), *New Introductory Lectures on Psychoanalysis*

"But I have had good reason for asserting that everyone possesses in his own unconscious an instrument with which he can interpret the utterances of the unconscious of other people."

Freud (1913), *The Disposition to Obsessional Neurosis*

"You will learn that the long and deeply brutalized man hates, in every relationship, the one who wants to pull him out of his condition, and treats him like an enemy."

Johann H. Pestalozzi (1781–87), *Leonard and Gertrude*

"Resistance is not everything, though it is a way of looking at everything."

Schafer (1973), *The Idea of Resistance*

ACKNOWLEDGMENTS

This book is dedicated to the therapists, supervisors, and patients who so patiently labored with me to understand and resolve my resistances to being a good therapist; to my mentors and colleagues of the Postgraduate Center for Mental Health who helped evolve my identity as a psychotherapist and psychoanalyst; to Abrahm Kardiner, who, in his kindly and scholarly manner, imparted an understanding of Freud to which few are privy; to Lia Knoepfmacher who ingeniously taught me by her example, love, and intuition; to Hyman Spotnitz who taught me, also by example, but with a freshness that brooked no deviation from integrity and basic care; to my colleagues at the Northern Westchester Center for Psychotherapy who helped refine my approach; to my patients who provided me the crucible wherein I could work out my ideas and who patiently and persistently taught me how to treat them; to my children, Gabrielle and Annette, who earnestly helped me become a better therapist and author; and finally to my wife, Simone, whose accommodations to my schedules, constant encouragement, professional stimulation, and loving concern provided me with the support much needed in writing a book that exposes so much of my professional life.

Croton-on-Hudson, N.Y.

I wish to extend my gratitude to Ethel Clevans, Leah Davidson, Everett Dulit, Arthur Feiner, Benjamin Margolis, Phyllis Meadow, Joseph Oelbaum, George Saltz, Hyman Spotnitz, Natalie Schwartz and Lewis Wolberg who gave so generously of their time to read and constructively criticize the manuscripts.

I also wish to acknowledge the intelligence, patience, and efficiency of Carol Clark during the seemingly endless revisions and typing of the manuscripts.

Grateful acknowledgment is made for permissions to reprint copyrighted material, as listed below.

Chapter 3 is based on Marshall, R. J., The Treatment of resistances in psychotherapy of children and adolescents, *Psychotherapy: Theory, Research and Practice,* 1972, *9,* 143–48, and is reprinted with the permission of The Division of Psychotherapy, American Psychological Association.

Chapter 4 is based on Marshall, R. J. "Joining techniques" in the treatment of resistant children and adolescents, *American Journal of Psychotherapy,* 1976, *30,* 73–84, and is reprinted with the permission of the Association for the Advancement of Psychotherapy.

Chapter 9 is based on Marshall, R. J. Countertransference in the psychotherapy of children and adolescents. In L. Epstein and A. Feiner (Eds.) *Countertransference: The therapist's contribution to treatment.* New York: Jason Aronson, and is reprinted with the permission of the publisher. The paper also appears in *Contemporary Psychoanalysis* 1979, *4,* 595–629 and is reprinted with the permission of the William A. White Institute.

Permission was granted by the publishers to cite from Bandler, R., & Grinder, J. *Patterns of the hypnotic techniques of Milton H. Erickson, M.D.* (Vol. I). Cupertino, California: Meta Publications, 1975.

Permission was granted by the Hogarth Press Ltd. for the citations from *The standard edition of the complete psychological works of Sigmund Freud.*

INTRODUCTION

This book is about the interlocking resistances of the patient, the patient's family, and the therapist and the means by which the resistances can be resolved. In the treatment of neurotic adults, the source of resistance to treatment had been placed within the patient. Similarly, in the treatment of children and adolescents, therapists worked with the intrapsychic resistances. The advent of child developmental studies and the child guidance movement shifted the locus of "blame" for lack of success in treatment to the parents, presumably the mother. Then, as therapists' attention was drawn to the family as a system, the resistance, lo and behold, was found in the family. Generated in the late 1930s, there was a slow movement that, accelerating in the 1950s, and mushrooming in the 1970s, spotlighted countertransference processes in the therapist which both hindered and helped therapeutic endeavors. Rather than seeing transference–countertransference and resistances–counterresistances in a disparate and disembodied manner, an attempt is made to discern, investigate, and resolve those interactional fields and gestalts of resistances and countertransferences that impede progress in treatment. This book also portrays patterns of resistances and countertransferences not only as impediments to treatment, but as crucial clues in determining etiology, maintenance, and eventual resolution of the resistances.

This book is about bridges and connections among seemingly disparate theories and therapeutic approaches. Many parochial clinicians and theorists may be offended *ipso facto* by any attempt to relate psychoanalytic theory to behavior theory or to see connections, for example, between Milton Erickson, Hyman Spotnitz, and Heinz Kohut. However, if we assume that these therapies and therapists have been successful in helping and healing patients, there are probably similarities among them. This book attempts to discern these similarities rather than emphasize the differences.

This book also attempts to recognize, understand, and resolve some of the contempt, anger, and harshness that therapists hold toward patients who do not proceed according to the therapists' expectations. Although experienced otherwise by therapists, resistances to therapeutic progress are neither "good" nor "bad." They are a phenomenon of human nature analogous to the forms of resistance manifested in nature such as heat and friction, which deserve scientific study. However, therapeutic resistances do induce emotions in therapists, which may subjectivize the field but which if properly understood, can facilitate the therapeutic flow.

This book is about "joining techniques," which are interventions used under other terms by a variety of therapies. Primarily affirming the right to resist, joining techniques simultaneously strengthen and resolve resistances. A central joining technique, "mirroring" or "psychological reflection," has wide theoretic significance and therapeutic application, and presents a promising conceptual avenue for understanding many complex psychological processes.

This book is about counterresistance which evolves from the therapist's countertransference. Therefore, countertransference is examined in detail and an analysis is made of the previous lack of attention to this critical area. Of the eight types of countertransference defined, one is seen to be of particular value in understanding the resistance–counterresistance field of interaction. This special countertransference consists largely of the efforts of the patient to communicate emotionally (on a preverbal level) with the therapist. This field is further complicated by the presence of the parents toward whom the therapist evolves countertransferential attitudes which, in turn, produce counterresistances.

This book explores Freud's writings on resistance and concludes, in line with his view of transference and countertransference, that he viewed resistance as both an impediment and a necessary and useful tool. Freud's technical approach is also dualistic: on one hand resistances are to be interpreted and resolved; on the other they are to be studied and supported until they are capable of being analyzed. Other psychoanalytic clinicians augmented but did not qualitatively change Freud's conceptions and techniques. Child therapists actively pursued the theory and approach to resistance analysis especially after 1965. Their contributions, sparked by Anna Freud, emphasized phase-appropriate interventions and the need to leaven interpretations with supportive activity.

This book examines Freud's direct contributions to the treatment of children, adolescents, and families. The emerging theme is that maturational influences must be combined with interpretative measures. In the review of the child and adolescent literature on resistance, one finds again the seeming dilemma between ego support and interpretation. With few exceptions, psychotherapists tend to support the defenses of preoedipal structures and analyze the reisistances of oedipal constellations. The ability to understand and respond appropriately to the patient's levels of functioning constitutes the greatest clinical challenge.

Chapter 1

ON THE HISTORY OF THE CONCEPT OF RESISTANCE

The concept of resistance and its history in respect to adult psychotherapy and psychoanalysis has been discussed by many authors including Glover (1955), Greenson (1967), Langs[1] (1976b, 1980), Menninger (1958), Rosenthal (1978), Sandler et al. (1973), Schafer (1973), Singer (1965), L. R. Wolberg (1977) and Wolstein (1964). No attempt will be made to review the total field which, to Freud in 1937, was "bewilderingly strange and insufficiently explored" (p. 241). Rather, a focused summary of the development of the concept of resistance is presented to provide the necessary background for an understanding of resistance as it has been used in child and adolescent therapy, family therapy, and as developed in this book.

Freud's Contributions to Theory

Freud, of course, was responsible for the discovery of the monumental concept of resistance. He noted its workings early

[1]Langs' (1981) significant contribution was received too late to be integrated into the manuscript.

in his clinical practice. In *Studies in Hysteria* (1895), he defined resistance as an opposition to or interruption of therapy. In particular, he portrayed resistance as a force in opposition to remembering; a ubiquitous and irresolute "enemy" to be "fought," "overpowered," "combatted," "melted," "broken," etc. A consideration of Freud's choice of verbs in discussing how resistances should be met, provides a measure of one orientation (termed "military" by Wolstein [1964] and "paternalistic" by Schafer [1973]) which he held over the course of his work. Initially, Freud saw resistances as a nuisance, then as "all the forces which oppose the work of cure" (1926, p. 223), which could range from "trivial dimensions" to "invincibility." Refining his notions of transference resistance, he discerned that resistances were inevitable, even necessary. In his ability to turn adversity to advantage, Freud discovered one of the benchmarks of psychoanalysis, namely, that resistances, if properly analyzed, could provide a reconstruction of the original trauma and the history of the development of the defenses and character structure. In reproaching the use of hypnosis, he (1905[1904]), stated

> it conceals from us all insight into the play of mental forces, it does not permit us, for example, to recognize the *resistance* with which the patient clings to his disease and thus even fights against his own recovery; yet it is this phenomenon of resistance which alone makes it possible to comprehend his behavior in daily life (original italics). (p. 261)

Thus, by 1904 Freud had established a dualistic concept of resistance as being a hindrance and a help in line with the mode in which he came to view transference and countertransference. Freud (1910[1909]) clearly related resistance to the original defensive constellation.

> The same forces, which in the form of resistance, were now offering opposition to the forgotten materials being made conscious, must formerly have brought about the forgetting and must have pushed the pathogenic experiences in question out of consciousness. (pp. 23–24)

Finally, providing the capstone in his advocation of resistance analysis, Freud (1916–1917) declared

> Resistances should not be one-sidedly condemned. They include so much of the most important material from the patients' past and bring it back in so convincing a fashion that they become some of the best supports of the analysis if a skillful technician knows how to give them the right turn. (p. 291)

Freud had generally equated defenses, based on repression, with resistance. But he found it necessary to distinguish more clearly between defense and resistance. Consequently, in 1926, he codified another important conceptual alteration, defining five types of resistance. The first was the resistance powered by the ego's need to protect itself by repression. Second was the resistance provided by the secondary gains of the symptoms that had become egosyntonic. Third was the transference resistance, in which the patient recreated the repressed in the therapeutic relationship rather than remembering. Fourth was the "id resistance" which, because of its biological roots, needed constant working through. Fifth was the superego resistance which originated from a sense of guilt or need for punishment, and opposed a successful cure. Freud (1937), in relating guilt, masochism, and the negative therapeutic reaction to the death instinct, deepened his concern about the power of the latter resistance and its amenability to analysis. In 1937, as if creating another category of resistance, he cited bisexuality as an idea against which some of the strongest resistances are evolved. In women, the wish for a penis is avoided while in men, the "repudiation of femininity" (p. 250) is central. Freud also conceived of a meta-resistance which he termed "a resistance against the uncovering of resistances," (p. 239) which reflects a resistance to the analysis as a whole.

As a theorist, Freud persistently worked at delineating resistances, describing their function and etiology, as well as relating them to the topographic, structural, economic, genetic, and adaptive aspects of psychoanalytic theory. As a clinician, he constantly worked at refining his techniques, searching for ways and means of resolving resistances. What was Freud's technical orientation toward handling resistances?

Freud's Contribution to Technique

As Freud (1895) recognized the patient's opposition to his cathartic "hands on" method, he passed through a stage where he used persuasion, exhortation, and "insistence" on remembering. His applying physical pressure on the patient's forehead with his hand developed into exerting "psychical influence" (p. 282). Although he periodically advocated the use of "force" or "pressure" in overcoming resistances, he did note that a resistance established for a long time "can only be resolved slowly and by degrees, and we must wait patiently" (p. 282). In his role as educator, he provided information and explanations about psychical processes as he attempted to induce collaboration (p. 282).

> Introducing the role of the therapist, Freud observed, "besides the intellectual motives which we mobilize to overcome the resistance, there is an affective factor, the personal influence of the physician, which we can seldom do without, and in a number of cases the latter alone is in a position to remove the resistance." (p. 283)

These statements presage Freud's penchant for working within the context of a positive transference. According to Freud, the therapist could act not only as an elucidator and teacher but could also be the confessor who sympathetically grants absolution.

Noting in italics that *"it is quite hopeless to try to penetrate directly to the nucleus of the pathogenic organization,"* (p. 292). Freud settled for working at the "periphery of the psychic structure" and "getting the patient to tell us what he knows and remembers." At this point Freud was still using the pressure techniques. It is likely that he gave up his physical pressuring before 1900 and dismissed the use of hypnosis in 1896.

Even as Freud slowly evolved his key notion of free association, he still approached resistance in an intellectual manner. For example, in 1904, he pronounced, "psychoanalytic treatment may in general be conceived of as such as a *reeducation*[2] *in overcoming internal resistances*" (p. 267) (original italics).

In the case of Little Hans, he (1909) continued his "reeducational" approach using the term "enlightenment" to characterize the information and interpretations provided by Hans' father.

In 1910, Freud (1910b) noted two important conditions for the "elimination" of resistances: (1) patients must be near the repressed material themselves; (2) the transference must be positive so that the patient will not leave.

In 1916, Freud posed and answered his own question,

> "How do we remove the resistance? In the same way: by discovering it and showing it to the patient. . . . interpret, discover and communicate . . . We expect that this resistance will be given up and the anticathexis withdrawn when our interpretation has made it possible for the ego to recognize it." (p. 437)

In extending his study of resistance to the realm of dreams, Freud (1923[1922]) took an unusually mild, almost casual approach to the resistances of the patient who opposed interpretation of dreams. ". . . one can feel confident that there is not much prospect of collaborating with the dreamer, one decides not to bother too much about it and not to give him much help, and one is content to put before him a few translations of symbols that seem probable" (p. 110). In discussing patients who doubt a great deal as a resistance, Freud advises against "shouting down" the patient, appealing to authority or arguing, but recommends, "The analyst too, may himself retain a doubt of the same kind in some particular instances" (p. 116).

In 1940, Freud underscored the analysis of transference resistance in reaching analytic goals. "We shall have struck a powerful weapon out of the hands of his resistance and shall have converted dangers into gains . . . [by] a careful handling of the

[2]Later translations indicate that the word "aftereducation" is more appropriate.

transference" which meant "enlightening the patient in the true nature of the phenomena of transference" (p. 177).

As late as 1940, and after 40 years of practice, Freud still perceived resistance as a grave danger to the course of analysis. He insisted that an unpleasant but necessary battle must be fought in which resistances are wrested from the patient by interpretations.

However, in the same summary, Freud casts resistances in the opposite light as he discussed psychotic states. ". . . we infer that the maintenance of certain internal resistances is a *sine qua non* of normality" (p. 161). Furthermore, he propounded the strengthening of a weak ego before the interpretation of resistances.

A View of Freud's Later Assessment of Resistance

Freud (1910a), became increasingly pessimistic and chagrined about the unyielding quality of certain resistances. In discussing the future of psychoanalysis, he sounded an alarm that has echoed in increasing amplitude ". . . no psychoanalyst goes further than his own complexes and internal resistances permit" (p. 145). He noted the obstacles of countertransference and counterresistance, yet acknowledged that the therapist's countertransference could be used in the understanding and reconstruction of the patient's unconscious. He did not follow up and expand his ideas about the positive aspects of countertransference in the manner that he pursued the value of resistance and transference. Although he (1913) declared, ". . . everyone possesses in his own unconscious an instrument with which he can interpret the utterances of the unconscious of other people" (p. 320), he saw countertransference and counterresistance as major hindrances to be "overcome" and over which "the therapist must rise." He gave no specifics; only the advice to conduct continual and deep self-analysis.

While it may be argued that Freud's "witch," metapsychology, prevented him from understanding and treating the narcissistic disorders, his pessimism about patients who refused to get well or who developed a "negative therapeutic reaction" may have led him to a reliance on metapsychological explanations that increasingly developed instinctual hues and faded into the obscurities of libido theory. Possibly, Freud applied psychoanalytic methods to patients who had narcissistic qualities undetected by him. Regardless, he (1917[1916–1917]) flatly declared that the narcissistic neuroses "can scarcely be attacked with the technique that has served us with the transference neuroses" (p. 423). He reasoned that the wall of narcissism was unconquerable because there existed "no capacity for transference" (p. 447). This type of reasoning later emerged in the analysis of children.

Evidence for Freud's discouragement abounds in *Analysis Terminable and Interminable* (1937). He concerned himself with the "constitutional" or genetic strength of the instincts and spoke of their "decisive" importance in the success of analytic treatment (p. 224). Emphasizing the importance of the physiological changes in puberty and menopause, Freud, after a startingly candid statement ". . . the whole field of inquiry is still bewilderingly strange and insufficiently explored" (p. 241), concluded in a paroxysm of despair and scientific obfuscation that we must find the answers in four inherited resistances: (1) "adhesiveness of the libido"—the slowness with which persons change their attitudes and alliances; (2) mobility of the libido—the rapidity with which persons shift their allegiances and involvements; (3) depletion of plasticity—similar to "resistance from the id," it is the inertia and rigidity in functioning; (4) the interplay between the death instinct and Eros. Freud provided no means by which these biologically rooted resistances could be broached, which in turn led to his consideration that analysis could be interminable.

Freud (1940[1938]) made his final and somewhat more optimistic statement about his technical stance toward resistances.

> The overcoming of resistances is the part of our work that requires the most time and the greatest trouble. It is worthwhile, however, for it brings about an advantageous alteration of the ego which will be maintained independently of the outcome of the transference and will hold good in life. (p. 179)

In the *Outline of Psychoanalysis,* Freud clearly outlined the technique of resistance analysis which is presented in the form of a dialogue.

If the first step is to strengthen the ego, "How is this accomplished? . . . Extending of its self-knowledge." "Accordingly, the first part of the help we have to offer is intellectual work on our side and encouragement to the patient to collaborate on it." (p. 177) After therapists gather information from free associations, transference phenomena, dreams, and parapraxes, and then construct the forgotten past, how do they use this information?

> But in all this we never fail to make a strict distinction between *our* knowledge and *his* knowledge. We avoid telling him at once things that we have often discovered at an early stage and we avoid telling him the whole of what we think we have discovered. (p. 178)

At what point are information and interpretations given?

> . . . it is not always easy to decide. As a rule we put off telling him of a construction or explanation till he himself has so nearly arrived at it that only a single step remains to be taken, though that step is in fact the decisive synthesis. (p. 178)

Suppose we proceed otherwise and provide premature interpretations?

> Our information could either produce no effect or it would provoke a violent outbreak of *resistance* (original italics) which would make the progress of our work more difficult or might even threaten to stop it altogether. (p. 178)

Given the arousal of resistance, what should the analyst do?

> With the mention of resistance, we have reached the second and more important part of our task. . . . [Because] the ego draws back from such undertakings [interpretation of defenses], which seem dangerous and threaten unpleasure; it

> must be constantly encouraged and soothed if it is not to fail us. (p. 178)

As interpretative work occurs simultaneously with strengthening the ego, what should the therapist anticipate?

> The further our work proceeds and the more deeply our insight penetrates into the mental life of neurotics, the more clearly two new factors force themselves in our notice, which demand the closest attention as sources of resistance. . . . They may both be embraced under the single name of need to be ill or to suffer. (p. 179)

How should the therapist approach this resistance? ". . . we are obliged to restrict ourselves to making it conscious and attempting to bring about the slow demolition of the hostile superego" (p. 180).

Are there other resistances?

> It is less easy to demonstrate the existence of another resistance, our means of combatting which are especially inadequate. There are some neurotics in whom, to judge by all their reactions, the instinct of self-preservation has actually been reversed. They seem to aim at nothing other than self-injury and self-destruction. (p. 180)

In general, what is the role of the analyst in the course of treatment?

> To start with, we get the patient's thus weakened ego to take part in the purely intellectual work of interpretation . . . (p. 181).
>
> We encourage it (the ego) to take up the struggle over each individual demand made by the id and to conquer the resistances which arise in connection with it (p. 181).
>
> We restore order in the ego by detecting the material and urges which have forced their way in from the unconscious, and expose them to criticism by tracing them back to their origin (p. 181).

> We serve the patient in various functions, as an authority and a substitute for his parents, as a teacher and educator [cf. 1895 statement re therapist function].
>
> We have done the best for him if, as analysts, we raise the mental processes in his ego to a normal level, transform what has become unconscious and repressed into preconscious material and thus return it once more to the possession of his ego (p. 181).

Freud, in conclusion, returns pessimistically to his dualistic energy model, wherein the balance of therapy is metaphorically attributed to the "bigger battalions" to whom God owes his allegiance.

CONCLUSION

Early in his clinical practice, Freud discovered the phenomenon of resistance. Consonant with his dualistic approach, two aspects of resistance are evident. The first is the "enemy" component that hinders free association, recall of memory, and opposes the process of cure. Freud's approach to this opposition was intellectual, belligerent, surgical, and catabolic. On the other pole are the functions of protection of the ego and communication of the development of the defense-resistance. Freud treats this side with the curiosity of a physician who studies the symptom for clues in determining the etiology of the dysfunction. He also approached the protective function with the respect of a supportive, understanding educator who was often the blank screen or mirror. To oversimplify, Freud seemed to take both an aggressive (paternal) and a nurturing (maternal) position toward resistance.

The "interpret" or "support" dichotomy has polarized the field unnecessarily into two camps: the purists who, probably working with highly selected, well-integrated patients, maintain that interpretation is virtually the only activity in which a therapist should engage; the therapists who, "working on the barricades" with more primitive patients tend toward supportive interventions and pragmatic solutions.

Throughout his career Freud seemed preoccupied with and extraordinarily puzzled by patients who frustrated his powerful intellect and fought his ministrations. He was successful in treating patients with oedipal or neurotic conflicts, but he increasingly despaired of resolving preoedipal or narcissistic resistances. At the same time, Freud reached deeper and more elaborately into the morass of instinct and libido theory—possibly in a search for his own preoedipal life?

Other Psychoanalytic Contributions to the Theory of Resistance

Other psychoanalysts have investigated resistance, but their contributions amplify and amend in minor ways rather than qualitatively change Freud's basic theory. Similarly, the approaches to resolving resistances were not markedly changed.

Glover's (1928[1955]) modifications and delineations are of value when seen in relation to his later discussions of counterresistance and countertransference. For example, he observed two types of resistances: obvious and unobtrusive (silent). The analyst usually meets the obvious resistances with ease except when the resistances happen to strike at a flaw in the therapist's makeup. The subsequent counterreactions disturb the treatment. The unobtrusive resistances are difficult to identify. The analyst is apt to meet them with "silent" counterresistances that are usually out of his or her awareness, and which confound treatment.

Glover also emphasized the functional aspect of resistances, lining them up with the different mechanisms of defense. He then proceeded to relate particular resistances to certain clinical syndromes: repression with hysteria; reaction formation, isolation, and undoing with obsessional states; projection with paranoia; and integration with depression. Finally, he underscored the significance of the transference-resistance and warns clinicians of their own potential for reacting emotionally to the patient's intensity and tenacity.

Resistance cannot be discussed without including the impact of W. Reich. Largely synthesizing and deepening the work of

Freud, Reich (1949) focused on the character defenses and resistances that hardened into an "armor," displayed themselves in everyday life, and emerged as "character resistances" in treatment. Reich's approach to resistance appears relentless, sometimes assaultive, but systematic. Noting that the analysis of resistances "cannot be taken up soon enough," he advised the therapist to select the predominant or "cardinal resistance," and confront the patient with it until the patient perceives it as ego alien and no longer an automatic functioning part of the personality. He was careful to point out several other principles of resistance analysis: (1) precedence must be given to those ego defenses closest to conscious awareness; (2) techniques of resistance analysis must derive from full understanding of the individual; (3) interpretation of resistance must occur before interpretation of content. That is, revelation of id material, or that against which the defenses are erected, must occur "much later" than resistance interpretation; (4) allow the transference (resistance) to come to affective fruition before interpreting.

Fenichel (1935[1953]),(1941) crystallized the classic psychoanalytic theory of technique regarding handling of resistance. He notes "the management of resistance and transference is the criterion for estimating whether a procedure is analysis or not" (p. 24). "Breaking" the resistance, primarily through "naming seems to us the *via regia.*" Fenichel regards interpretation as a monolithic approach to resistances and perhaps has done more than anyone to promulgate the general idea that interpretation is the only legitimate activity of the psychoanalyst. For example, he declares, "the ideal analytic technique consists in the analyst's doing nothing other than interpreting and the ideal handling of the transference too, consists in not letting oneself be seduced into anything else" (p. 87). Any other activity "always involves the danger of joining in the acting out of the patient" (p. 88). Although he advocates "bribing" and "convincing" the patient, these are presumably nonanalytic techniques.

Federn (1952) accepted Freud's dynamic model and saw the emergence of psychotic material as a failure in the defense-resistances. His experience led him to conclude that analytic procedures used in the treatment of neurotics "must be abandoned or used in homeopathic doses" (p. 155) in the treatment of manifest and latent psychosis. To avoid decompensation and reestablish defense-resistances he counseled: (1) abandon free association "because enough unconscious material has been provided to the therapist *and* patient"; (2) "abandon analysis of the positive transference" because positive transference is essential for treatment; (3) "abandon provocation of transference neurosis" because it develops into a psychotic transference; (4) "abandon analysis of resistances which maintain repression" because the freeing of repressions produces more psychotic material. What is left for the analyst to do? In distinguishing between resistances to recovery and resistances to emergence of unconscious material, Federn suggests working with "real objects" (p. 156) in reducing fear, guilt, and illusions.

Roy Schafer (1973), in his attempt to facilitate the communication of psychoanalytic concepts, analyzes Freud's notion of resistance. Schafer prefers the use of the verb to the noun because the noun tends to reify the concept. The dualism of the concept emerges in Schafer's "action language" definition: "Resisting is engaging in actions contrary to analysis while engaging in analysis itself" (p. 265). In an interesting psychosocial analysis of Freud's perspective on resistance, Schafer indicates that because Freud generally took a patriarchal view of the world and saw in it warring elements, he approached in a patriarchal way that which opposed him. Schafer points out the "negative," pejorative, and aggressive connotations of psychoanalytic language and suggests that analysts develop affirmative and positive language particularly in their approach to resistances. Schafer's analysis leads one to speculate that attention to oedipal factors such as castration and homosexuality could represent a paternal orientation. Interpretation could then be an aggressive phallic intervention, especially if one considers the belligerent verbs that Freud used.

Baranger and Baranger (1966) define resistance as a functional sequence of processes in patients: (1) feeling threatened by an unconscious danger; (2) refusing to regress; (3) maintaining a schizoid splitting for their defense; (4) isolating part of their egos to keep an eye on the imminent danger; (5) defending the frontiers of their internal worlds; (6) protecting themselves from encroachment by the analyst. Emphasizing the interactional role of the analyst, they indicate that the state of resistance of the patient corresponds to feelings of noncommunication within the analyst.

Langs (1980), placing the concept of resistance into his adaptive-interactive field theory, refines the definition of resistances. "They are best conceived of as all efforts, behavioral and communicative to oppose or interfere with the process of insightful, adaptive psychoanalytic care, as derived from factors with the patient, analyst and their interaction" (p. 50). Langs "reaffirms" the centrality of resistance in analytic work, but extends the concept by integrating therapist variables and the analytic "frame."

Klauber (1968) attempts to differentiate between resistances and "legitimate defenses." In this important distinction, he advocates an assessment of the defense-resistance structure and analysis of only those that contribute to impeding the treatment. While Klauber applied this principle to the treatment of adults, it seems especially relevant to the treatment of children and adolescents.

Compared to the Freudians, other analytic schools have accorded resistance very general use and/or have adapted it to their particular metapsychologies and philosophies.

Rank (1945) took strong issue with Freud's view of resistance, and believed it was a function of the analyst's resentment of the patient not performing as expected according to the Freudian design. Contrary to Freud, Rank believed that "resistance" to the therapist's expectations actually was a sign of progress, self-direction, independence, and a manifestation of the patient's "will." Opposition to the therapist was therefore considered to be a favorable sign and not an interference. Threads of his positive orientation to resistances run through the Philadelphia School of Social Work and the works of Taft, Allen, and Haley.

Trying to correct a Freudian notion, in 1912 Adler (Ansbacher, 1956) declared that transference resistance begins very early in treatment and that the therapist may not recognize the signs until the patient has terminated. Adler listed the following as "subtle expressions" of resistance: "expressions of doubt, criticism, forgetfulness, tardiness, any special requests by the patient, relapses after initial improvement, persistent silence, as well as stubborn retention of symptoms" (p. 337). He also included "hearty friendship and peace" as marking no progress. The more obvious forms of resistance were direct hostility to the therapist which reflected the patient's depreciatory and superiority strivings. Adler sharply differed from Freud in conceptualizing the motivation for resistance. "It is the depreciation tendency which underlies the phenomenon Freud described as resistance and erroneously understood as the consequence of the repression of sexual impulses" (p. 337). In 1929 Adler shifted the motivational underpinning of resistance toward a broader social base.

> "The so-called *resistance* is only a lack of courage to return to the useful side of life. This causes the patient to put up a defense against treatment for fear that his relation with the psychologist should force him into some useful activity in which he will be defeated" (original italics) (p. 338).

In his early approach to resistance Adler, taking a belligerent direction, advocated "disarm" the patient and "take the wind right out of the patient's sails." He also seemed to want to avoid the mobilization of resistance and to prevent the patient from depreciating the therapist. In line with Freud's style, he sought to "explain" the patient to himself and provide insights. Adler, too, was struck with the force of resistance to the therapist's interventions, "Every therapeutic cure, and still more, any awkward attempt to show the patient the truth tears him from the cradle of freedom from responsibility and must therefore reckon with the most vehement resistance" (p. 27).

As Adler shifted his theoretical emphasis, his handling of resistance took a milder turn. For example, in 1929 he noted "We must never force a patient, but guide him very gently towards the easiest approach to usefulness. If we apply force, he is certain to escape" (p. 338). Later, he described his benevolent interaction with an assaultive girl "not of great physical strength." In putting up no resistance and "looking friendly" when the girl hit him, he surprised her, "taking away every challenge." "She broke my window and cut her hand in the glass. I did not reproach her, but bandaged her hand" (Ansbacher, 1956, p. 136).

Melanie Klein devoted little space to resistance in her writing. She insisted that resistances are to be overcome by interpretations. She recognized that some interpretations arouse resistance and anxiety, but the subsequent interpretations resolve the impasse. She finds that the positive transference of the child and the cooperative feelings of the parents are essential to ameliorate the child's resistances.

Arlene Wolberg (1973), in discussing her approach to borderline patients with her projective technique, advocates an avoidance of confrontations and interpretations until the patient is ready to handle the attendant anxiety. *"The aim of the treatment is to help the patient let up on the creation of defenses rather than force him by premature confrontations to increase his defenses"* (original italics) (p. 207). Wolberg prefers to deal first with "areas of least resistance." For example, while permitting the patient to talk about the "other person" Wolberg will analyze in an "off target" manner those aspects of the patient which are projected into the "other person" without making direct reference to the patient. This aspect of technique is similar to Spotnitz's (1969) penchant for working first with object-oriented as compared with ego-oriented material.

Horney (1942) defines resistance as "the forces that oppose liberation and strive to maintain the *status quo*" (p. 267). She describes three types or styles of resistance: (1) open fights against the provoking problem; (2) defensive emotional reactions to the analytic situation or analyst; (3) defensive inhibitions and evasive maneuvers. Her major approach to resistances is through free association while holding the positive attitude that resistance is an "organic development," not a proof of "stupidity or obstinacy." The drive toward self-actualization also tends to overcome the forces of resistance.

Daniels (1980), in line with Horney's positive view, states that resistance is

> "an inescapable property of the human condition. Personal growth defines itself in its struggle against internal resis-

> tances just as light defines itself against a backdrop of darkness. One cannot be conceived without the other" (p. 53).

As an analogy for resistance in natural phenomena, electrical resistance could be seen as the *sine qua non* of heat and light. Similarly, resistance in mechanics is termed friction, without which we could not walk, a wheel could not roll, nor could a screw hold in place.

A major theoretic and technical approach to resistance, especially with schizophrenics, delinquents, and "hard-to-treat families," has been evolved over the past 30 years by the "Modern Psychoanalytic" school whose mentor is Spotnitz. His conceptualization of resistance rests on classic psychoanalytic ground while emphasizing its protective, survival, and communicative functions. For Spotnitz, resistance is

> "prominently identified with the early defenses patterned by the ego in the interests of environmental mastery and psychological survival. These protective devices are activated in the treatment situation by transference, and when their mobilization interferes with communication they are identified as resistance. In short, defenses activated by the charge of transference become resistances" (p. 78).

He notes that resistance operates on different levels of personality functioning: the lower the level, the more difficult the communication and the less responsiveness there is to interpretations. He treats resistance nonjudgmentally: "As the best adjustment the patient was able to make at the trauma level, resistance is simply a force that needs to be recognized and dealt with throughout the treatment" (p. 79).

Recognizing Freud's five types of resistances, and emphasizing the transference resistance, he conceives of five other resistances empirically rooted in the clinical process and sequence. According to their priority they are: (1) treatment destructive resistances—similar to the "obvious" resistances of Glover, they include tardiness, missed sessions, and other behaviors that threaten the continuity of therapy. Included in this category are external resistances with which Freud did not deal, and internal resistances; (2) status quo or inertia resistances—usually evolving after the first six months, the patient pleasantly drifts in the analytic current; (3) resistance to analytic progress—the patient demonstrates reluctance about exploring new emotional territory and the prospect of change; (4) resistance to teamwork and cooperation—the patient is loath to react, to give up narcissism and react to the analyst as an object in a mutual relationship; (5) resistance to termination—the patient declines functioning as an autonomous person.

Two other resistances must be resolved to facilitate progress: (1) the narcissistic transference resistance—a resistance occurring early in treatment wherein patients, assuming their typical narcissistic defense against attacking the object, continue to be self-preoccupied, attack themselves, and otherwise adapt their pathology to the treatment milieu. The concept of the narcissistic defense, which is the centerpiece of Spotnitz's theory of schizophrenia, assumes major significance in the modern psychoanalytic approach to resistance especially since it evokes countertransference; (2) the object-transference resistance—occurring later in treatment, schizophrenic patients begin to recognize and use therapists as objects. When a negative object transference resistance is operating, therapists remain under attack which represents a release of hatred for their objects or themselves. Similarly, in a positive object-transference resistance, the patient may idolize the therapist in a manner reminiscent of Kohut's idealizing transference.

Spotnitz (1969) explains his noninterpretative approach to these resistances in detail. The following is a succinct categorization of interventions without the rich clinical data provided by Spotnitz: (1) commands—usually used to mirror the tyrannical and demanding patient; (2) questions of three types—factual; object-oriented questions about the outside world, the analyst, etc.; ego-oriented questions about the patient; (3) explanations—brief answers given only to facilitate communication; (4) ego-dystonic joining—the therapist mirrors behavior that the patient finds objectionable in himself or herself; (5) ego-syntonic joining—the therapist mirrors behavior that the patient finds agreeable and comforting; (6) motivational interpretations—parsimonious explanations given at the level of the patient's understanding in order to facilitate communication and only at the patient's request.

Nonpsychoanalytic Positions

Nonpsychoanalytic schools generally disregard the phenomenon of resistance. For example, behavior therapy ignores the concept, although individual behavior therapists have discussed resistance (Weinberg and Zaslove [1963], Crisp [1966], D'Alessio [1968], Feather and Rhoads [1972a,b], Rhoads and Feather [1972]. There seems to be a gap in the literature from 1973 to 1981. In general, as behavior therapists meet resistance, they remove the blocks by applying principles of behavior therapy. The intellectual, educational, almost exhortative approach is reminiscent of Freud's early efforts to induce collaboration in the patient. For example, Hersen (1971) states, "Generally, however, resistance is met with simplified lectures in operant conditioning principles in conjunction with positive, nonpunitive suggestions for altered parental response." (p. 123) Behavior therapists may attempt to prevent the formation of resistances by telling ". . . the patient at great length about the power of the treatment method, pointing out that it has been successful with comparable patients and all but promising similar results for him, too" (Klein et al., 1969, p. 262). Patients are provided with a detailed learning-theory formulation of the etiology of their problems and are given a straightforward rationale for the way in which the specific treatment procedures will "remove his symptoms" (Klein et al., 1969, p. 262).

Behavior therapists have not incorporated the concept of resistance because of the unobservables inherent in the psychoanalytic concept. But since resistant behavior *is* observable, it is not clear why behavior therapists have not addressed it to any significant extent. Hersen (1971) speculates that the manner in which cases are reported by behavior therapists limits discussion of resistant behavior. D'Alessio (1968) believes that training in behavior modification precludes exposure to psychoanalytic training and experience.

Client-centered therapy also has had no room for the concept of resistance. This exclusion appears to be a function of the paramount and guiding principle of self-actualization. Rogers (1961) has portrayed human beings as innately good, and as constantly and naturally striving for awareness and a realization of their capacities. Emphasis is on potentiating upward growth of the individual rather than on removing those factors that prevent development. Contrast this outlook with Freud's (1913) statement, "Education seeks to ensure that certain of a child's [innate] dispositions and inclinations shall not cause any damage either to the individual or the society" (p. 330).

Roger's model derives from a phenomenological field approach that tends to be ahistorical and does not subscribe to the deterministic genetic and energy concepts of psychoanalysis.

A psychoanalyst writing about Gestalt Therapy, Appelbaum (1979), finds that gestalt therapists "declare resistance out of court" in their attention to the "here and now." "Instead of analyzing resistance, gestalt therapists assert that the patient needs his resistance—but as a conscious option, rather than an unconscious compulsion." (p. 482). Appelbaum believes that "going with the resistance" is a "powerful technique" that provides the following advantages: (1) stubbornness and negativism are neutralized through offering the patient an acceptable amount of independence and control; (2) in recognizing the need for resistance, the therapist's human understanding and acceptance becomes apparent to the patient; (3) avoiding countertransference binds associated with "moving the therapy"; (4) avoiding judgmental behavior and thus a transference trap; (5) avoiding casting the patient into a passive role by getting rid of the resistance; (6) preventing the patient from feeling attacked by the therapist and deprived of his defenses and symptoms (cf. Ekstein's [1966] space child who said he would always blame his therapist for taking away his space fantasies).

The work of Bateson, Jackson, M. Erickson, and the more recent contributions of the Palo Alto group as well as Haley's Strategic Therapy is referred to as the communications approach to psychotherapy. Their main contribution to the theory of resistance is the idea that resistance can be *used* to therapeutic advantage. Resistance, when first observed is considered to be an obstacle, but communication therapists immediately search for a way in which it can be utilized.

Erickson in 1967 recognized the profound resistance of some of his hypnotic subjects. He interpreted the resistance not as opposition *per se* but as "an expression of an actual willingness to cooperate in a way fitting to her (the patient's) needs" (p. 19). Erickson defined resistance as "an unconscious measure of testing the hypnotist's willingness to meet them halfway instead of trying to force them to act entirely in accord with his ideas" (1952, p. 19).

In 1959, Erickson evolved "utilization techniques" in which he refined his ideas that resistances can be accepted and used to gain cooperation. Expanding this positive technique to clinical problems, he would redefine a patient's pathological preoccupation with a perceived defect so that the patient came to use and value that technique. Erickson also saw a communicative function in resistance. In discussing openly hostile and defensive patients he advised,

> "This attitude should be respected rather than regarded as an active and deliberate or even unconscious intention to oppose the therapist. Such resistance should be openly accepted, in fact graciously accepted, since it is a vitally important communication of a part of their problems and often can be used as an opening into their defenses" (1964, p. 472).

For example, a patient belligerently scorned and defied Erickson to treat him, yet ordered Erickson to treat him saying, "So, get a move on." Erickson, with a casual tone and smile replied,

> "O.K. shut up, sit down, keep your damn mouth shut and listen; and get it straight, I am going to *get a move on* (using the words of the patient's own request) but *I move just as slow or as fast as I damn please*" (my terms for the acceptance of his request for therapy were phrased in his own language) (p. 473).

Watzlawick (1978) in discussing the use of the patient's resistance prefers the concept of "reframing" the symptom. For example, in the presence of a rebellious teenager, Watzlawick will tell the parents that their son "is not really insolent, but is reacting to a deep-seated, existential fear of growing up and of losing the comfortable safety of childhood" (p. 145). Watzlawick feels that this statement mobilizes the teenager's resistance to prove that he is mature. Secondly, the parents become inclined to be more tolerant, thus lessening the boy's push against them. The use of paradoxic prescriptions are also used to advantage in resolving resistances.

Conclusion

As suggested by E. Singer (1968), the various theories of resistance were derived not only from scientific observation, but from the theorists' scientific and cultural *Zeitgeist,* their personality, and their view of human nature and motivation. Several major currents flow through the various theoretical seas. One trend essentially ignores the phenomenon or attempts to "bypass" it (behaviorism and gestalt). A second view, as exemplified by Rank, finds resistance a favorable and healthy sign. The communications school sees resistance as being useful. A fourth view, typified by Rogers, Horney, and Spotnitz, perceives the protective, survival, and homeostatic functions in resistance. The fifth position, provided by Freud, pessimistically portrayed resistance as opposing cure and being rooted in instinctual and biological processes. Adler also lent a malevolent cast to resistance by attributing its motivation to a need to depreciate others. Yet Freud also viewed and treated resistances positively as he spelled out their protective and communicative function.

Given a phenomenon that opposes cure, as well as prevents the realization of a person's growth potential, most systems of psychotherapy and psychoanalysis have evolved a concept called resistance, which serves several functions. Some clinicians pit themselves against resistance in zealous attack, others "let it be," while others attempt to use it in the service of cure.

The position of this book is that resistance is an intervening variable which is useful in understanding certain patterns of clinical behaviors correlated with "no progress," "negative therapeutic reaction," and therapeutic failure and which in turn are closely connected with the symptoms and everyday functions of the person. These behaviors contain messages which, if properly understood, reveal the source and the reason for the development of the therapeutic and personal difficulties. Once this configuration of cause and effect is understood, the therapist must evolve a plan to resolve the therapeutic resistance, which in turn leads to personality change.

Chapter 2

ON RESISTANCE IN THE TREATMENT OF CHILDREN, ADOLESCENTS, AND PARENTS

FREUD'S CONTRIBUTION TO CHILD, ADOLESCENT, AND FAMILY THERAPY

Despite the fact that Freud did not work with children, adolescents, and their families, save for the indirect treatment of Little Hans in 1909, he momentously influenced the field of child and family therapy through his formulations extrapolated from adult analyses. The frequently revised *Three Essays on the Theory of Sexuality* (1905) is the centerpiece of Freud's theory of childhood development. Klumpner (1978) provides a succinct organization of Freud's writings about adolescents. Although Freud wrote little about child therapy and the family, the following quotations are illuminating, anticipate major developments, and are central to the therapeutic approach discussed here.

In a candid manner, Freud (1917[1916–1917]) revealed his fear and ignorance of patients' parents. "In psychoanalytic treatments the intervention of relatives is a positive danger and a danger one does not know how to meet" (p. 459). In a discussion of "external resistances" he acknowledged the role of family members in sabotaging treatment.

> No one who has any experience of the rifts which so often divide a family will, if he is an analyst, be surprised to find that the patient's closest relatives sometimes betray less interest in his recovering than in his remaining as he is. (p. 460)

He absolved the therapist of blame in the treatment failure of a woman whose husband opposed therapy and in the case of a daughter whose mother saw analysis as a threat to her relationship. Freud turned from dealing with these family influences for he saw the task of psychoanalysis as the resolution of inner resistances. This position apparently has had great impact on many workers who were led to believe that the removal of intrapsychic conflicts and resistances was the primary, if not the sufficient, therapeutic task. But Freud did note, "The external resistances which arise from the patient's circumstances from his environment, are of small theoretical interest but of the greatest practical importance" (p. 459). His focus on internal resistances coincided with his major conceptual turn in 1905 when he chose to see reports of seduction as determined by internally produced fantasies rather than external events.

In a later work, he (1933[1932]) addressed himself again to the problem of resistant parents and the nature of resistance in children.

> The internal resistances against which we struggle in adults are replaced for the most part in children by external difficulties. If the parents made themselves vehicles of the resistance, the aim of analysis and even the analysis itself—is often imperiled. Hence it is often necessary to combine with a child's analysis a certain amount of analytic influencing of his parents. (p. 148)

Recognizing the feedback of knowledge and technique between the realms of adult and child analysis, and the necessity for flexibility in the analyst, he continued,

> On the other hand, the inevitable deviations of analysis of children from those of adults are diminished by the circum-

> stances that some of our patients have retained so many infantile character traits that the analysts (once again adapting himself to the subject) cannot avoid making use with them of certain techniques of child-analysis. (p. 148)

Freud commented that a child is "a very favorable subject for analytic therapy" with results that are "thorough and lasting." He noted that techniques of treatment must be different for child and adult because ". . . he possesses no super-ego, the method of free association does not carry far with him, transference (since the real parents are still on the spot) plays a different role" (p. 148).

In discussing the treatment of children in his preface to Aichhorn's *Wayward Youth,* Freud (1925b), emphasized that certain educational steps must be integrated into the process because children are not small adults and do not have the maturity and the "psychical structures" to warrant or withstand analysis.

> A child, even a wayward and delinquent child, is still not a neurotic; and after-education is something quite different from the education of the immature. The possibility of analytic influence rests on quite definite preconditions which can be summed up under the term "analytic situation"; it requires the development of certain psychical structures and a particular attitude to the analyst. Where these are lacking —as in the case of children, or juvenile delinquents, and, as a rule, of impulsive criminals—something other than analysis must be employed, though something which will be at one with analysis in its *purpose.* (p. 274)

Freud made a distinction between "analysis" and "education" that was echoed in Anna Freud's work and has, in turn, reverberated throughout theoretical and clinical chambers.

Presumably Freud implied that the child be approached so as to strengthen its ego, modulate the demands of the superego and id, and help the child mature. What did Freud mean in advocating the development of a "particular attitude" on the part of the analyst? Presuming that he was referring to Aichhorn's work, he may have alluded to Aichhorn's manner of establishing a dependent, narcissistic relationship or transference and then using that position as a base for later analysis.

Freud (1926) reaffirmed that a maturational education or experience must precede or be integrated into the analytic process. "In the child's interest, it is true, analytic influence must be combined with educational measures" (p. 215). In the same paper, he viewed the treatment of children not only as a maturational and curative process but as a "prophylaxis" against illness in later life.

Finally, in an incomplete paper (1940[1938]b), he discussed the concept of splitting of the ego. A 3- or 4-year-old boy, threatened by castration, "artfully" managed to continue masturbating by developing a fetish.

THE FIRST RESISTANCE

The anläge of resistance appears to be in the "No" phenomenon discussed by Spitz (1957,1965). Noting that deprived infants did not engage in the same negative head shaking as normal infants, Spitz, upon further investigation, concluded that negative head shaking and in particular, the verbalization of "No" are not only major developmental milestones, but the latter manifests the third "organizer of the psyche" which significantly influences future development.

> *The acquisition of the "No" is the indicator of a new level of autonomy of the awareness of the "other" and of the awareness of the self; it is the beginning of a restructuralization of mentation on a higher level of complexity; it initiates an extensive ego development in the framework of which the dominance of the reality principle over the pleasure principle becomes increasingly established* (original italics). (1957, p. 129)

Propelled by the frustration evoked by the negative head shaking and prohibitions of the mother, the 15-month-old child identifies with and imitates the mother. Instead of being forced back into a passive position by the prohibitions to initiative and activity, and faced with a conflict between satisfying wishes and risking loss of the object and its love, the toddler identifies with the aggressor. One might add that the "No" preserves the emerging ego *and* the object. In one magnificant gesture, the child forestalls regression to passivity, substitutes words for action, preserves the object, and identifies with part of the mother. Spitz believed that the "No" represents the first abstract communication wherein physical action is replaced by a message transmitted across a distance.

Spitz (1965) surmised that the 15-month-old understands only two affects in the other: "for" and "against." The child develops the primitive idea, "If you are not *for* me, you are *against* me." If this premise is true, and given the child's feeling that the mother is not "for" him or her, it follows that negativism will be profound, especially if the child continues to identify with a perceived negative mother. Also, in order to prevent the child from forming characterological negativism, he or she must develop an optimal feeling that the mother is "for."

Spitz's findings and speculations contribute significantly to a theory of resistance. The first autonomous resistant behavior occurs at 15 months and is a reaction to the prohibitions of the mother who seeks to curtail the child's activity. The reaction of the child is defensive, growth-producing, compromising, and protective of ego and object. Moreover, early resistant behavior may be a function of the amount of "for" and "against" feeling evoked by the mother.

Therapists' emotional reactions to the phenomenon of resistance may relate to the manner in which one views the "No." Some theoreticians and clinicians tend to value the oppositionalism, seeing it as a valid protest against an arbitrary encroachment on the growth of the person. Others tend to view the negativism as a rigid obstinate foreclosure to outside influence and change. That is, some are "for" and some "against."

The Problems in Investigating Resistance in Children and Adolescents

While resistance has held a central position in theories and techniques of adult psychotherapy, child therapists have paid relatively less attention to it. This deficit needs some exploration as does the dearth of literature in the area of countertransference to youthful patients (cf. Chapter 9).

Melanie Klein's virtual dismissal of resistance in her interpretative work may easily account for her students' neglect of the area. Anna Freud's (1926b), (p. 46) statement that "transference neurosis" could not be established with children, probably discouraged investigation of the area. If a child could not develop a transference neurosis, consequently a transference resistance could not evolve. When she (1965) revised her opinion, indicating that transference neurosis could occur but not the equal of adult transferences, analysts devoted considerable interest to transference and resistance (Abbate, 1964; Casuso, 1965; Harley, 1961; Kay, 1971; Lilleskov, 1971; Ritvo, 1978; Scharfman, 1978; Van Dam, 1966).

The delay in achieving a clear and comprehensive study of resistance is due to the ways in which resistances are manifested by children and adolescents. The variety, intensity, subtlety, fragmentation, and diffusion of resistances is so great as to lead to emotional reactions and countertransference that lead therapists away from, rather than toward the relentless and frustrating challenge. The more primitive the child, the greater the task. Child therapists probably experience the "bewildering strangeness," but few have had the capacity of Freud to attempt unswervingly to understand and master the new territory and write about the tribulations of the therapy.

A. Freud's Comparison of Resistances in Adults and Children

A. Freud (1965), of course, is one who has not turned from the task. She believes that "the forces opposing analysis are, if anything, stronger with children than with adult patients" (p. 33). Her comparison of an analysis of an adolescent with running next to an express train clearly reveals her perception of the emotional involvement necessary to conduct therapy with adolescents.

She asserts that children share all of the resistances of adults as well as obstructions specific to their age:

1. The child does not enter treatment under his or her own free will and since there is no contract, the child is not bound by rules.
2. The child has no long-term view of the future gains which ordinarily mitigates the discomfort of therapy.
3. Acting out tends to be more pronounced.
4. Since the ego is more immature, the defenses are tighter.
5. Ego resistances are increased because primitive defenses operate alongside the more mature ones.
6. Since the child's ego sides with his or her resistances, the child is more apt to leave therapy. Thus, the therapist must engender the parent's support.
7. There is a greater tendency to reject the past in latency and adolescence.
8. The child has a great tendency to externalize.
9. The child is more egocentric and narcissistic and is less apt to establish object relations.
10. The secondary process is weaker.
11. The sense of time is not as developed.
12. Genital phenomena are apt to be perceived pregenitally.
13. There is a relative lack of introspection.

Flight into Health and Transference Cure

Resistances in the forms of "flight into health" or "transference cure" are common reactions. Several clinical pictures occur early in the treatment process. Initial appointments are made and broken. Upon inquiry, the therapist is told that the problem has improved or even disappeared. In other instances, the child's parents or family appear for the initial interview and again the therapist is informed that the problem has improved to the extent that therapy does not appear to be necessary. The symptoms have greatly diminished but the underlying dynamics and pathology remain the same. One of the more frequent causes of diminution of anxiety and the amelioration of symptoms is that the child, and sometimes the parents, fantasize that their suffering will soon end due to an alliance with the therapist. Children and adolescents have frequently advised me that they felt better or the family problem seemed to lighten when the parents had committed themselves to a decision to obtain assistance. A frequent report is that after the initial telephone call, which is an overt act toward receiving help, the family finds a "miraculous" reduction in the problem. The "improvement" seems to be of such a magnitude that they excuse themselves from the initial appointment or arrive at the first consultation questioning what they are doing there or lukewarmly describing "past problems."

In more complex cases, however, the prospect of assistance tends to induce anxiety and fear because of a sense that the equilibrium, however insufferable, will change for the worse.

Oremland (1972), in reviewing the phenomena of flight into health and transference cure in individual treatment, cites the following differences: flight into health is composed of "sudden, global, massive repressions and suppressions of the pathological feelings, actions, and activities which occur very early in the therapy, sometimes even before the first appointment is kept" (p. 64). Entailed may be a mixture of splitting, denial and projection with a focus on incidents rather than object relationships; transference cure is considered more complex in that it involves: (1) fear of relationship with the therapist; (2) identification with the therapist; and (3) the wish to please the therapist.

Transference Resistance

One of the most important resistances is contained in the transference resistance. Seemingly, a transference resistance can be evolved only in a transference neurosis. The classic psychoanalytic literature indicates that a transference neurosis rarely occurs in the treatment of a child. Fraiberg (1955) stated that only four cases had been reported in the literature, and the transference neurosis occurred two to four years into the analysis. How then can we conceptually account for the intense, repetitious resistance behavior while the child seemingly is in transference or at least seems to have a deep relationship to the therapist that seemed to be based on the parental ties? Stone (1967) provides a way out of this conceptual dilemma by suggesting that transference may occur on three *levels.* The first is the "primordial," wherein the patient is driven by "parasymbiotic" needs and generally seems to want to recreate the symbiotic relationship with the mother. The second level is the "transitional object transference" wherein the analyst and analytic situation represent a transitional object to the patient. The third level is the "mature" transference which seeks individuation and reality.

Lilleskov (1971) attempts to reserve the concept of the transference neurosis for those conditions where, in the course of analysis, the original *oedipal* conflicts are displaced onto the analyst. Lilleskov defines four types of transference manifestation and then distinguishes the following processes as simply processes in the relationship—not transference phenomena.

(1) Therapist is undifferentiated from the primary object. In this relationship there is no repression and no conflict. This appears to be akin to the autistic stage of development.
(2) Therapist as an object undifferentiated from the self—a narcissistic transference. This is a common type of transference and is not clear why Lilleskov calls this a narcissistic transference but not a transference.
(3) Displacement of a current conflict with the person of the analyst.
(4) Generalized reactions expressed toward the analyst.
(5) Expression of character traits in the analyst.
(6) The real relationship.

Attempts to reserve the term "transference resistance" for neurotic phenomena seem somewhat strained and artificial. My experience with severely disturbed patients has taught me that they are capable not only of intense transferences but also of equally strong transference resistances. It seems sensible to talk of different types of transference resistances such as neurotic, narcissistic, or autistic, depending on the status of the development of object relations. As soon as one talks of defense, one must talk of resistance when in the therapeutic situation. This book focuses on transference resistances that fall in the narcissistic range and resolve into the neurotic.

Resistances to the Transference

Every patient seeks to recreate the troublesome past while seeking to avoid it. Every patient studies the therapist to determine whether or not the therapist can be helpful. What seems to keep patients in treatment is their idea that *at the same time* they can work maximally toward recreating and resolving past developmental failures or conflicts while minimizing the hurt from affects that attended the earlier maturational failure.

Many patients spontaneously reestablish that early predicament. For example, the neglected child who has developed little sense of self will come into the room, sit down, and stare at the therapist or appear to be disinterested in the therapist. Countertransference reactions may then dominate and counterresistance action may disturb the patient's essentially cooperative and communicative position. Many therapists mistakenly condemn behavior as resistant, i.e., opposition to the authority, power, and competence of the therapist, while overlooking the communicative function of the behavior. Thus, the resistance of the patient, incorrectly interpreted, produces a resistant therapist.

Patients resist forming certain types of resistance. For example, narcissistic patients resist forming an object transference, but cling to their narcissistic transferences. The therapist must resolve the narcissistic resistance to leaving the narcissistic transference and developing an object transference. Sandler et al. (1975) discourage interpretation of resistance to transference in adolescents. "Adolescent patients . . . can often stay in treatment when this [displacement of transference] is tolerated by the analyst and not interpreted as a resistance to experiencing the transference in the present" (p. 437).

Daniels (1969) sees the analysis of two early resistances—defense against the transference and defense transference—as the chief work in the first phase. These two resistances are the forerunners of the defense against establishing the transference neurosis. Working with neurotic adults, Daniels believes that these resistances can be met by "clarifying, educative and interpretative comments" (p. 1012) while establishing the working alliance.

It is hypothesized that resistance to establishing a transference occurs only when the patient validly surmises that the therapist cannot be helpful and/or will be hurtful. Given a patient with a degree of striving toward growth and a reasonably competent therapist, transference reactions automatically develop. When resistance to the transference seems to occur, one must consider the *therapist's* reluctance to have the patient develop a transference.

Defense–Resistance or Developmental Arrest?

Anna Freud (1970[1957]) describes the difficulty in treating the child whose development has been arrested in the need fulfillment or anaclitic level. That child develops an anaclitic object transference which she found shallow, egocentric and one-sided.

> "The patient is demanding, insatiable, and intolerant of the ensuing frustration of his transferred wishes. He is unable to stand either the unpleasure or the anxiety aroused by interpretations or to make any efforts to respond to or work through interpretations" (p. 7).

Stolorow and Lachman (1980) argue persuasively for a differentiation between psychopathology based on defenses against intrapsychic conflicts and that predicated on developmental arrests at prestages of defense. They draw attention to two types of processes that may result in a final common pathway of symptoms. In either case, patients evolve resistances to the examination and treatment of their condition. One may infer that the type of resistance based on conflicts yields more easily to interpretation. The resistances evolved by the developmentally arrested person may need a different kind of intervention.

Kohut (1977) also suggests that there are two types of resistance that require different interventions:

> Some of the most persistent resistances encountered in analysis are not interpersonally activated defenses against the danger that some repressed psychological ideation will be made conscious by the analyst's interpretations or reconstructions; they are mobilized in response to the fact that the stage of the analyst's empathic echo or merger with the patient had been skipped over. In some analysis—though by no means in all—the analyst will even have to realize that a patient whose childhood self-object had failed traumatically will require long periods of "only" understanding before the second stage—interpretation, the dynamic-genetic explanations given by the analyst—can be usefully and acceptably taken. (p. 88)

Interpretation Versus Support of Resistance

The type and intensity of the resistances are not only age-specific (physical and psychological) but are, in turn, related to the diagnosis. These determinations are crucial in planning treatment strategies. For example, A. Freud (1965) recommends "truly analytic measures" of transference and resistance interpretations for a neurotic child. For borderline children, interpretations of resistance are useless, whereas clarifications of internal and external dangers are called for. For more psychologically arrested children, she suggests a "corrective emotional experience."

In interpreting resistances, she fully expects that the ego will not collapse under the "onslaught." In those cases where there is danger of a decompensation, she suggests that the modifications suggested by Aichhorn are appropriate.

Taft's (1962) avoidance of interpretation and appreciation of resistance, derived from Rank, ring out from her statement written in 1933:

> . . . Resistance too, is evident enough here on every page, but it is never handled by interpretation nor is any attempt

> made to break it. Rather it is met as far as possible, frankly and without denial or counterresistance in feeling, even when its practical execution must be checked, and with a real appreciation of its inevitability and positive value as an expression of the child's will, however, negatively put. (pp. 200–201)

Sylvia Brody (1961), in discussing transference resistance in prepuberty, spoke of the effects of interpretation on narcissistic characters.

> Yet however tactfully interpretation is offered it makes for more difficulties with children of all ages than with adults because . . . of the essentially narcissistic investment of the child's defenses. (p. 255)

She further advocates that ". . . much care must be taken to nourish the transference resistance" and that "much delicacy" be exercised in the interpretation of play.

Harley (1970) describes an awkward spiral in the therapy of an adolescent who suffered "a painful narcissistic hurt" from an interpretation and felt further "criticized for feeling criticized" when the analyst acknowledged the boy's hurt. In reaction, the analyst found that he had begun to gratify the adolescent, but "finally found the proper analytic ground" (pp. 108–109).

Fraiberg (1955), commenting on the "precarious balance of pubertal ego," felt that analysis was contraindicated in puberty and that "exceptional demands in the analytic method" were to be made if pubertal children were to be treated appropriately.

> The aims of puberty and the aims of analysis are hostile to each other. At a time when the ego must strengthen its defenses against the powerful resurgent drives analysis must disturb the defensive structure in order to do its work. (p. 264)

Fraiberg then compares the therapist to a tightrope walker who treads a line between gratification and hurt. She counsels, "at the beginning of treatment, almost any interpretation, no matter how little, how superficial, constitutes a threat to the patient" (p. 276).

Kut Rosenfeld and Sprince (1965) sharply define the problem with borderline children. "At first many of us tried to deal with this problem [anxiety] by interpretation in the usual way, but found that the anxiety seemed to increase" (p. 512). They cite the disadvantages of interpretation with the borderline child; it affects development of transference, blocks affect emergence, and pushes ego development ahead of libidinal development. Their discussion of the use and timing of interpretation with borderline children is particularly constructive.

Ritvo (1978) reiterates a basic psychoanalytic position regarding treating children: the psychoanalytic process is limited by the child's developmental status and must be adapted to the development of the child. He suggests that direct interpretations break off fantasy play not because of the child's resistance, but because the child cannot comprehend and carry out the stages of abstraction, conceptualization, and generalization. Resistance to interpretations is examined as a function of lack of maturity rather than the presence of defense-resistances.

In discussing a type of prelatency child in whom ego imbalances and ego defects occur, Weil (1973) discourages analytic methods and recommends "preparatory educational therapeutic help which aims at making up for early interactional failures and at stimulating ego growth and better integration" (p. 299). The ego-strengthening process should be conducted by someone other than the person who later analyzes the child.

Fergelson (1977) provides qualifications about interpretations to a child. He feels that interpretations made within the context of the play and about the play figures are more efficacious than direct interpretations about the child. As the play leads to feelings experienced by the child, then interpretations are appropriate.

Harley (1961) and Fraiberg (1955), among others, have made the point that specific types of resistances relate to certain maturational phases. Although this seems to be true for neurotic children, it may be that the characterological defense-resistances override the usual age-specific behavior in more disturbed children. Freud (1925b) suggested this point in his statement, "Analysis has shown how the child lives on, almost unchanged, in the sick man . . ." (p. 273).

From a sociological point of view, Durkin (1967) portrays interpretation as serving several functions in a children's treatment center: 1) objectify and mitigate the emotional impact of the children's behavior; 2) control of staff; 3) sophisticated name calling; 4) *ad hominum* arguments; 5) control of children; 6) emphasize sick role; 7) outlet for aggression.

S. R. Slavson (1952) recognized the consequences of premature and inappropriate interpretation. "Interpretation of defenses presents its own peculiar and very serious risks. Any premature threat to defenses creates anxiety and resentment that may well destroy the transference relation." Before interpretation

> . . . one must be certain that (1) the transference is positive and firmly established, (2) that the ego is strong enough to give up its defenses or at least to examine them, and (3) that they are recognized as no longer a function of the personality, but rather vestiges of the past and a continuation of habit patterns. (p. 190)

Berta Bornstein (1951) contributed significantly not only to the field of child therapy but especially to the understanding and use of resistance and defense analysis with the latency child. Because she saw the latency child as being in "precarious equilibrium" she advocated the following:

> Because the child battles against his impulses and needs to keep up his defenses, we must be particularly careful to respect his resistance and to work through his defenses before we approach the material which is warded off. . . . Defense analysis is more complicated in the analysis of children than in that of an adult. . . . The utmost care has to be exercised in the analysis of latency to strengthen weak structures and to modify those which interfere with normal development. (p. 285)

Kestenberg (1972) underscored an important and common resistance in young children—their wanting to remain loyal to their parents. She submitted that the child needs permission from the parents in order to talk about the family.

Sarnoff (1976), in his comprehensive work on latency, advocates flexibility according to the child's cognitive, dynamic, structural, and developmental levels. Noting the "calm, pliability and educability" of the latency child, he attempts to support the defenses and structures that induce those characteristics. The ability to fantasize is a central trait of the latency child and therefore is a pivotal issue in the child's psychotherapy. Sarnoff notes that fantasy can be used as a resistance, as a major source of information about conflicts, and can function as a necessary base for the child's growth. Stereotyped and repetitive fantasies are resistances that must be analyzed. In handling this resistance, he maximizes the child's changes and/or unique contributions by questions, asking for drawings, cutouts etc. When the child drifts from the work, Sarnoff readdresses himself to the fantasy until the conflicts are analyzed.

Gardner (1979) reviews the common forms of resistant behavior and briefly reviews five therapeutic approaches: psychoanalysis, activity play therapy, release therapy of D. Levy, relationship therapy of F. Allen, and client-centered therapy. He describes eight specific techniques using drawings, drama, boardgames, and toys.

Gardner (1975) has devoted an entire book to various psychotherapeutic approaches to the resistant child. Forsaking traditional methods, but from a broad-based psychoanalytic frame of reference, he provides a practical guide to structuring interviews with resistant children. Supplying typescripts of interviews, he guides the reader through the various innovative "games" that have emerged from his extensive clinical experience. Kritzberg (1975) has also provided a valuable psychoanalytic approach to resistant children through his "structured therapeutic game method."

Rinsley (1980), in describing his work with severely disturbed adolescents, catalogs verbal and nonverbal resistances:

(1) Identification with the staff
(2) Egalitarianism
(3) Flirtatiousness—seductiveness
(4) Oversubmissiveness

(5) Persistent avoidance
(6) Scapegoating
(7) Outright rebelliousness
(8) Transference splitting
(9) Somatization
(10) Peer age-caricaturing
(11) Clique formation
(12) Craziness and pseudostupidity
(13) Intellectual pursuits
(14) Flight

Rinsley uses Bowlby's stages of infantile mourning as his model for resistance. Three distinct stages of protest, despair, and detachment are frequently manifested by the adolescent when hospitalized and separated from the parents. The protest stage reflects the patient's initial resistance to treatment; the despair corresponds to the subsequent depression where new introjects must be assimilated otherwise the detachment stage, signaling chronicity, will occur.

Rinsley places the twin fears of undergoing change and abandonment at the root of all resistances which, in turn, are defenses against depression. The depression is a function of internalized aggression and the terror of emptiness of internal objects.

Rinsley notes that when patients can say that they hate, without fear of reprisal from the therapists, they can begin to experience love. Rinsley, as well as Masterson, vigorously confront the adolescent with the initial resistances. Since the therapy proceeds in a hospital setting, the behavioral reactions of protest and despair can be safely contained. Their approach to resistances is suitable only for an institutional program due to the collapse of inner controls from confrontation and interpretation.

Kernberg's (1979) approach to patients 15 years and older emphasizes the need for an accurate diagnosis between normal and neurotic identity crisis, and borderline personality manifestations. The borderlines are characterized by identity diffusion (lack of integration between self and object representations), primitive defenses centered around splitting, and the maintenance of reality testing. Cautioning against the use of projective identification by adolescents, Kernberg seeks to analyze with the adolescent the cultural stereotypes into which the therapist is cast. In general, Kernberg advocates interpreting the primitive transferences of the borderline in the "here and now" because they represent the main resistances. The therapist helps the less severely disturbed adolescent to resolve the normal development task with a combination of expressive and supportive psychotherapy. Since Kernberg's series of patients tend to be older adolescents and young adults, his interpretative work, which is reminiscent of Fenichel's, may be better tolerated by their stronger egos.

Kut Rosenfeld and Sprince (1965) noted that their study group on the treatment of the borderline child "heatedly discussed" the appropriateness of interpretations versus ego-supportive measures. The group established that it was not a question of one approach being better than the other. The issue settled around the "balance, timing and personality of the therapist."

Conclusion

The dichotomy in approach (interpret or support the resistance) remains an issue in the literature. One of the reasons for the continuation of the problem is the lack of consistency in diagnostic criteria. That is, one person's "borderline" may be another's "narcissistic disorder" or "identity disorder." Perhaps the stricter definitions provided by *DSM-III* will help us label our patients with greater reliability and consistency.

Besides the confusion engendered by lack of clear diagnostic criteria, the differing arguments presented by psychoanalysts lead one to recognize our relative lack of knowledge of prestages of defense, preoedipal, or preverbal stages. Certainly, researchers such as Bowlby, Escalona, Spitz, Brody, Piaget, the Murphys, and Mahler have contributed much to our understanding of these early times, but there has been insufficient integration of theories of psychoanalytic psychotherapy with the vast efforts in cognitive, linguistic, and developmental psychology. Hunt (1979) uses 215 references in his review and synthesis of studies of early experi-

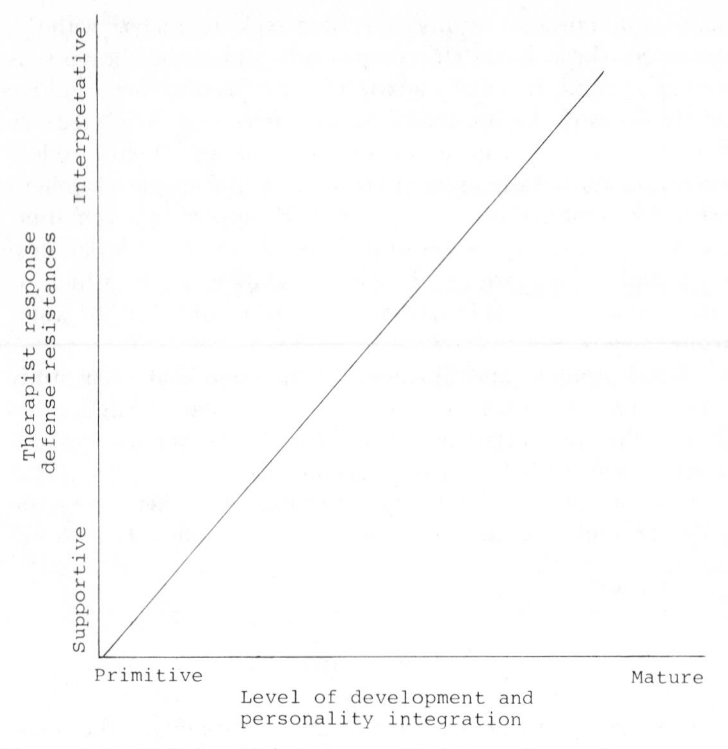

Figure 2–1 Relationship of personality integration and therapeutic approach

ence on psychological development. Especially useful are his summaries of studies relevant to psychoanalytic theory. However, the absence of such names as Mahler, Brody, and Escalona suggest that the task of synthesis is greater than Hunt's encyclopedic knowledge. A specific gap in this field is between psychoanalysis and workers such as Kagan (1978) who mount considerable evidence against the idea of continuity between early infantile–childhood states and adult personality and behavior. If we are to assume that borderline, narcissistic, and psychotic disorders hark back to early developmental eras, the field should establish more empirically validated models of infantile structure and function, which may be related to subsequent clinical behavior.

Given interclinician reliability in diagnosis and a valid developmental model, great differences will remain in approach to patients. Ekstein and Friedman (1971) provide a clue to the difficulty in selecting the most appropriate means of resolving resistances, particularly those of childhood psychosis: "Resistances all too often lie in the therapist rather than in the patient in adapting the techniques of classical analysis to the special needs of these extremely variant disorders" (p. 297).

Finally, we must question and reexamine the distinction between those interventions termed ego-supportive and educative and those termed confrontational and interpretative. Interpretations can be ego-supportive, but not all ego-supportive techniques are interpretations. Moreover, there may not be interpretation *per se* but types of interpretations, i.e., resistance-supportive and resistance-destructive.

The position of this book is portrayed in Figure 2–1. The more primitive the organization of the personality, the more supportive of defense-resistance the therapist should be. The more mature the personality, the more the therapist can remove defense-resistances. The following chapter describes approaches to children and adolescents whose personality development has been arrested or has regressed to preoedipal levels.

Chapter 3

RESISTANCE
Definition and Interventions with Joining Techniques

Resistance is conceptualized as an intervening variable (MacCorquodale and Meehl, 1948) and can be defined in terms of its antecedent and consequent conditions. The latter are fully observable, while the former must be deduced from clinical data. Defining resistance in terms of its antecedent and consequent conditions provides a more operational, rigorous, and scientific manner of examining resistance.

The Consequent Conditions

The consequences of resistance are manifested in varied forms. The general form is a diminution in the patients' verbalization of the story of their lives. In the case of children whose ability to verbalize is limited, resistance is seen as an arrest in the communication of the life story through words or play.

No attempt will be made to list resistances because their number are infinite and variegated according to the individual clinical situation. However, certain signs of resistances do coalesce into categories: (a) long silences, especially occurring over a number of sessions; (b) repetitive themes; (c) stereotyped and shallow themes; (d) a real threat to termination of therapy; (e) sustained intense emotional reactions within the therapist; (f) increase in acting out; (g) increase in symptoms; (h) deviations in the contract about time and fees.

The Antecedent Conditions

The antecedents of resistances are much harder to specify because they usually have occurred early in life, hence are unobservable except in symbolic form, acting-out, dreams, free associations, play, or from the reports of alert parents. The antecedents of resistance exist on a continuum from the most primitive and preverbal to the most sophisticated and verbal. The resistances usually coincide with the types of character defenses which, in turn, indicate where in the person's development the trauma or conflict occurred. Many researchers refer to "early" or primitive defenses such as denial and splitting, differentiating them from later and more mature defenses such as sublimation and repression. The antecedents of resistance also rest on the object relations. For example, the narcissist will establish narcissistic resistances. In general, patients will attempt to act out their history in the form of resistances rather than remember.

In the therapeutic situation, the therapist can discern some triggering events leading to the activation of a resistance. Vacations, cancelled appointments, and other external events may mobilize resistances. However, in a more psychoanalytic setting, where external cues are diminished and the transference develops, therapists must rely upon their powers of observation as they track patients' free associations or play sequences.

Metapsychological Classification

Taking a more systematic view, it seems possible to classify resistances according to psychoanalytic metapsychology.

Structural – Id, ego, and superego resistances as outlined by S. Freud (1926).

Genetic – Resistance can be seen in terms of the temporal origin of the development and transformation of related defenses. Conflicts at various psychosexual levels yield specific defense-resistance as discussed by S. Freud, Glover, and especially by Anna Freud (1936).

Economic – Some estimate can be made of the intensity and strength of various resistances. Hartmann (1950) believes that "numeration" or quantification is not possible and that terms such as "more," "less," "greater," "fewer," etc. are appropriate.

Topographic – Resistances can be divided into conscious, preconscious, and unconscious.

Dynamic – Since the phenomena of resistance imply conflict, the resistances may be categorized as follows: id–ego; id–superego; ego–superego.

Adaptive – Resistances can be seen as maintaining stability and homeostasis, providing protection, and otherwise having survival value for the organism.

Intervention

Resistances, when based on defenses evolved well after the preverbal level, can be met successfully with clarifications, confrontations, and interpretations. When resistances to treatment clearly reflect functioning stemming from a preverbal era, I believe that the classic psychoanalytic interventions have little utility, and, in some instances, can be damaging, especially to children, adolescents, and those with weak or immature egos. Joining techniques oriented toward supporting *and* resolving narcissistic resistances are the approaches of choice.

Joining Techniques

A series of techniques or interventions have been evolved by a number of clinicians to deal with the treatment-resistant preoedipal, preverbal, or "hard-to-treat" patients. They have been termed "joining" techniques.

The history of the development of these techniques has been told by Feldman (1978) and Strean (1970). The techniques are associated with those therapists who align themselves with Paradigmatic Psychotherapy (Nelson, 1968) or Modern Psychoanalysis (Spotnitz, 1976). These workers found joining techniques successful in the early stages of treatment of treatment-resistant families, schizophrenics, and delinquents who were functioning at primitive preverbal levels. Margolis (1981) provides an extended definition and description of joining techniques while Adams (1978) applies these techniques and strategies to psychoanalysis of drug addicts.

The following clinical vignettes provide a feel for joining techniques, after which the theory and rationale are explained.

Affirmation

Affirmation reflects an orientation pervading all the joining activities and treatment in general. Affirmation denotes the acts of recognizing, acknowledging, accepting, validating, and valuing the communications of the patient. The therapist directs affirmations toward the patient as a whole, but in particular to impulse, affect, and defense-resistance. Frequently the therapist must make a sharp distinction between affirming a patient's acts and the expression of thoughts, feelings, and fantasies. The latter, which constitute "talk," are virtually always affirmed, whereas actions may constitute acting out instead of remembering. The word affirmation is also chosen because Freud (1925a) saw it as "a substitute for uniting—belongs to Eros" as compared to "negation—the successor to expulsion—belongs to the instinct of destruction" (p. 239). Affirmation connotes a merging, loving quality that may be contrasted to interpretation which sometimes connotes an analytic–catabolic process that seeks to dispel and destroy defense-resistances.

Affirmation conveys to patients that the defense-resistances will not be opposed, interpreted, or removed until they are ready to yield the defensive position for a more flexible and favorable stance. One patient phrased his impression of the joining therapist, "You always manage to find the silver lining in that terribly dark cloud."

The particularly melancholic appearance of a schizoid, uncommunicative 13-year-old boy prompted me to remark about his mournful look. Don unexpectedly recited a brief dream of the previous night wherein he found himself crashing an automobile into an abutment. As we discussed the meaning of death and suicide to him, he assumed his typical affectless position, said that he had no feeling about dying, and refused further discussion. I told him that he had a very valuable asset in his detached attitude toward death. He looked quizzically at me because when I had previously confronted him with his detachment, I had communicated a negative valence. I told him that I was associated with a psychiatrist who was trying to help people who knew they were dying of incurable diseases. I went on to describe the terrible fear and distress of patients and staff and indicated that if they could know his devices of detaching himself from his feelings, he would contribute considerably to the comfort of these persons. He was interested enough to cooperate with me in spelling out in detail the psychological and behavioral operations he used to distance himself from his feeling such as, "keep busy," "be scientific," "tackle impossible problems," "think that life is worthless." We were then able to trace the history of these defenses. At about this time, he became a part of a theatrical–discussion group that helped him further value and use his feelings.

Don's parents wanted neither marriage nor children. Don was a very quiet baby who was entrusted to the care of many babysitters. He was continually exposed to the parents' incessant arguments and rages. Quite early in life, he had learned that feelings of any sort led to hurt or danger. As he developed, his occasional attempts to contact and relate to his parents were met with criticism, interminable lecturing, or simple withdrawal. When he was brought for treatment, Don's detachment was a source of anxiety and a focus for attack by his parents. The therapeutic intervention was probably successful because it affirmed a resistance that previously had been under attack, and it was presented in a credible manner consistent with his own and his parents' scientific, detached attitude.

Satiation

Bill was an extremely passive and seemingly easy-going 13-year-old who appeared very anxious to please. His typical character mode was to ingratiate himself to others and then frustrate them. He characterized himself as an "allergy child" and was able to spell out in some detail, but without affect, the history of his allergies. He also indicated that he was having some difficulty in reading and math, for which he was being tutored. He perceived no real problems in his life—the allergies were being treated medically and the school problem was being remedied. He then lapsed into building models and fixing toys while maintaining virtual silence. When asked to talk, he would nod, smile, and answer monosyllabically.

In the face of his defensive eagerness to please, I began a series of reasonable requests which he promptly and pleasantly agreed to, but equally reliably, neglected to carry out. I then confronted him with a series of unreasonable requests such as bringing me a ham and cheese sandwich for lunch. After three weeks of rationalizing his lack of action, he appeared with the promised sandwich. When I upped the ante to a steak sandwich, he squirmed, faltered, and apologized that he could not accede to my request.

As Bill continued to act compliantly, and in line with his compulsive fixing and cleaning in the playroom, I praised him and I asked him to bring from home a pail, mop, and soap to wash the floors and walls. Again, he benignly acquiesced in word, but failed to keep his promise session after session. In an increasingly irritated tone, I accused him of being unreliable, frustrating, forgetful, etc. As he fended off this pseudoattack smilingly with denial and rationalization, he began to recognize my excessive demands and reliance on him. He slowly and fearfully began to object in an emotional manner, more appropriate to the situation. He became more comfortable in revealing his rage toward me by demanding things from me and by calling me mean, cheap, dictatorial, etc. At about this time the parents reported that Bill had become more argumentative at home, but more reliable. The school also reported that he had erupted a few times at his peers, was less often a scapegoat, but was more of a loner.

When his parents became aware of my outrageous demands and Bill's compliant reaction, they were helped to see that Bill's do-nothing behavior and occasional temper tantrums were related to his unexpressed resistance to their stringent demands and expectations.

This technique used may be termed satiation of the resistance, in that the therapist sets up a situation where patients compulsively use their defense-resistance in a way that allows them to see the inappropriateness of their response, and which then allows the expression of the underlying affects, conflicts, and concerns.

In Bill's case, the therapist was also mirroring the behavior of the parents in order to reactivate the nuclear problem.

Bill was the son of a retired Army sergeant who apparently was skilled in the use of passive–aggressive techniques as an adaptation to his career. Bill learned his father's defensive mode well as he attempted to cope with his tyranny. The frequent absences of the father during Bill's childhood induced the mother to rely heavily on Bill, who responded with passive–aggressive behavior.

Satiation and Mirroring

One of the more succinct illustrations of the use of satiation and mirroring in resolving a resistance involved a borderline 5-year-old boy who spent most of his initial sessions counting. Fortunately, he could barely count past 10. At one point I asked him if I could count also. With his affirmative answer I began counting. At first patient, and aping my numbers, then fidgeting about, he finally exploded as we reached 531 "Stop that counting and let's do something else!" Occasionally he would lapse into his obsessional counting but as I joined him or did my own counting, he would cease. We could probably plot an extinction curve of his counting as a function of the increase in my counting.

The mirroring and satiation helped to evolve a narcissistic transference and to insinuate the therapist into a symbiotic relationship with this boy who was in a highly symbiotic relationship with his mother. The technique was used to resolve the resistance yet reassure the boy that he (and the therapist) could use an obsessional defense at any time.

Ordering or Prescribing the Resistance or Symptom

Prescribing the symptom, which is an extreme form of a joining technique, was introduced by Dunlap (1928), who wanted to motivate an oppositional patient to do something by a negative suggestion.

Frankl (1959,1960) uses "paradoxical intentions" to treat a variety of disorders. For example, to a man fearful of perspiring, Frankl advised the patient, "in the event that sweating should occur, to resolve deliberately to show people how much he could sweat." (p. 125) Frankl attempts to replace the fear with a paradoxical wish.

In treating a bookkeeper whose writer's cramp seemed to produce a suicidal depression, Frankl recommended, "instead of trying to write as neatly and legibly as possible, to write with the worst possible scrawl." He was advised to say to himself, "Now I will show people what a good scribbler I am! And at the moment in which he deliberately tried to scribble, he was unable to do so." (p. 127)

Frankl tries to rationalize his procedure as fostering a self-transcendence or a "self-detachment inherent in a sense of humor." That is, he tries to get patients to laugh at themselves and their neuroses.

Watzlawick et al. (1967), seeing "prescribing the symptom" as part of a "therapeutic double bind," provide several vignettes. One, taken from Jackson (1963) describes Jackson's insistence that he and a paranoid patient search every nook and cranny in the office that might reveal a microphone the patient thought existed. After that experience that patient began talking about his relationship with his wife, where he apparently had reason to be suspicious. "By teaching him to be more suspicious, the therapist, while joining in with the patient's paranoid tendencies, is forcing him to notice more about his relationships with other people" (p. 306)

By insisting that the patient be suspicious, the therapist combats a pathological inner directive to be naïve and overlook obvious and unpleasant messages, particularly as they occur in the double bind. "By joining the inquisition, he is providing the patient with companionship. He is also serving as a model, demonstrating that there is more to be found out; and he helps the patient to keep from being defensive about his relative ignorance." (p. 307) Certainly this tactic keeps the patient from being defensive about his symptom. Jackson cautions the therapist to be sincere in teaching the patient to be suspicious.

Watzlawick et al. cite another case, that of a woman whose incapacitating headaches communicated, "Help me, but I won't let you." Her psychiatrist indicated that since no treatment had helped her, her condition was irreversible and hopeless. Angry at this explanation, the patient attacked the uselessness of psychiatry. However, a week later she announced that the pain had retreated considerably. "At this the psychiatrist showed great concern; he criticized himself for not having warned her beforehand of the possibility of such a temporary, purely subjective lessening of the pain, and expressed his fear that the pain would now unavoidably return in its old intensity" (p. 247). He inveighed her to abandon hope of improvement and to learn to live with her condition.

> "From this point on her psychotherapy took a rather stormy turn, with the psychiatrist becoming more and more skeptical about his usefulness to her because she would not accept the 'irreversibility of her condition' and the patient angrily and impatiently claiming constant improvement" (p. 247).

The technique, interpreted in the light of present theory, is clearly a joining of the woman's resistance to being cured. When the patient, in her oppositional style, fought the psychiatrist, her resistance and defense resolved so that she could go on to explore other aspects of her life. Moreover, the freedom she had to attack the therapist seemed to reduce her narcissistic defense and lessen the attack on her ego.

Les, a highly resistant 9-year-old, whose alternate aggressiveness and detachment bewildered his parents, also posed a treatment problem because of the destructive and assaultive behavior in the sessions. As I became more aware of his extremely contrary nature while I tried to set limits, I ordered him to act in a destructive manner. Behind a barrage of "Who says so?" "Who's gonna make me," etc., he behaved in a pleasant manner, but lapsed into silence. I then ordered him to maintain his silence, at which point he launched into a series of reproaches, arguments, etc., which revealed important material and provided grounds for discussion. Later, when I ordered him to speak unpleasantly to me and not about nice things, he spoke of the fun of his vacation.

The technique used here approximates Spotnitz's (1969, p. 183) "commands" and may be termed "prescribing the resistance" in that the therapist literally orders the patient to exercise resistance. Prescribing the resistance may be best used with negatively suggestable persons. These are persons whose characterologic mode of response is "No." An important distinction should be made between prescribing the resistance and prescribing the symptom or the defense. It seems far safer and manageable to resolve the resistances than to try to handle the defenses and symptoms occurring outside the treatment session. Note should be made that in the cases presented here, the therapist dealt with the resistant behavior demonstrated *in the session.* Changes in defensive behavior *outside the session* were discussed only hypothetically.

Sam was a 10-year-old whose treatment began to slow appreciably. He began a series of resistances after announcing that he wasn't going to say anything more about his life. When he reiterated his unwillingness to talk, I said (in essence), "Sam, you've really told me a tremendous amount about yourself in a short period of time. I think you deserve a vacation in talking about yourself. So now tell me what kinds of things you can do in order to avoid talking about your life." I also indicated to him that I thought he was an "expert" in thinking up ways of avoiding talk. I enjoined him to tell me any conceivable ways of avoiding talk so that I might recognize those ways with other children. He readily revealed all of his ploys, such as going to the bathroom, taking a walk, and playfully suggested some resistances reserved for the future, such as playing games and going shopping for games. At this point I suggested to him that there probably were good reasons for his not wanting to talk, that he should really talk if he wanted to be helped, but that it was okay if he didn't talk. Sam then ventured some complaints and feelings about his parents, about which he felt guilty.

Mirroring, Echoing, and Psychological and Behavioral Reflecting

An 8-year-old boy, referred for academic underachievement and inordinate dependence, repeated the same inadequacy, helplessness, and demandingness in the therapy sessions. His persistent whining, requests for toys, assistance in building models, and seeking new objects continued for months. As I became more aware of my feeling of powerlessness in coping with him, I began acting in a helpless and hopeless manner and pleaded for assistance. At first, the boy became irritated with the therapist's immobility and then became very encouraging, helpful, and soon was acting in a self-assertive, independent manner. The moment I displayed any competence, he would become negativistic, move away, and begin a series of insatiable demands. This interaction served as a base for a discussion of his fears of being abandoned when acting in an independent manner. When his mother, in adjunctive counseling, noted a sharp decrease in her son's demands and tantrums, she was introduced to the idea of mirroring his demands. When she reflected some of his tantrums, he laughingly exclaimed,"You've been listening in on what Dr. Marshall does."

This case demonstrates a straightforward mirroring or reflection of the defense resistance. The therapist simply acted out the resistance of the patient. Note that the choice of defense-resistance to mirror was based on the helplessness experienced by the therapist.

Mirroring is an extremely important and powerful intervention which deserves special consideration. Darwin (1893) noted that his 9-month-old son displayed considerable interest in a mirror, and would turn toward his image when his name was called.

Of interest is Dian Fossey's field work (1970,1971) with the uplands gorilla. Unable to approach the apes close enough for needed observation, Fossey found that systematic imitation of their movements evoked a quietness and tolerance in the gorillas that allowed a closer approach.

> "I tried to elicit their confidence and curiosity by acting like a gorilla. I imitated their feeding and grooming, and later, when I was sure what they meant, I copied their vocalizations, including some startling deep belching noises. The gorillas responded favorably." (1970, p. 51)

At one point after Fossey imitated a gorilla, he seemed to imitate her. "It was not clear who was aping whom." (1971, p. 577) Whereupon, the great ape approached Fossey and touched her hand.

In summarizing the self-recognition studies with animals using mirrors, Lewis and Brooks-Gunn (1979) conclude that "No primate species other than the great apes has been found to exhibit self-recognition, even after thousands of hours of mirror experience" (p. 19).

The use of mirrors and instant print cameras by anthropologists is relevant. The general report is that when preliterate people see themselves for the first time, considerable affect is aroused. Usually surprise and fear resolve into pleasure and laughter. Foreign diplomats are now carefully tutored in the customs, mores, and nonverbal communications of the country to which they are assigned in order to facilitate favorable relations. "When in Rome, do as the Romans" makes good diplomatic and psychological sense.

Winnicott (1971) maintains that *"The precursor of the mirror is the mother's face"* (original italics) (p. 111). He argues that for babies, the mother's face is the first object differentiated from themselves. Therefore, the mother's facial expressions are of prime importance to the baby. When a "good enough" mother looks at her baby, *"what she looks like is related to what she sees there"* (original italics), as compared to a mother who is preoccupied or reflects her own mood when she looks at the baby. Winnicott postulates a need to be reflected which, when satisfied, leads to maturation and when frustrated may lead to pathology. He goes on to generalize about the process of psychotherapy, "Psychotherapy is not making clever and apt interpretations; by and large it is a long-term giving the patient back what the patient brings" (p. 117).

Piaget (1962), in his observations of mutual reciprocal imitation in child and adult, indicates that being imitated is a *necessary* preliminary to learning to imitate. He suggests that at the earliest sensorimotor stages of development, the infant's capacity to respond imitatively can only be mobilized by the mother's imitative activity. The significance of imitation for Piaget is that it "effects the transition from sensory–motor to representational behavior" (1969, p. 301).

Lending credence to Winnicott's and Piaget's arguments are the findings of Meltzoff and Moore (1977) who, in controlled experiments, demonstrated that an 8–12-week-old infant imitates expressions such as lip protrusion, mouth opening, and tongue protrusion.

Since Fout's (1972) work, several groups of experimentalists have investigated the effects of imitating infants, children, and adults. A general finding is that the experimental subjects are not only more responsive to the imitator, but they tended to imitate the imitator to a significant degree. In clinical research, Kauffman et al. (1975) demonstrated that imitation of a 7-year-old retarded child whose eating habits were inappropriate, drastically reduced the offensive behavior. Kauffman et al. (1977) imitated the unpleasant appearing tongue protrusions of a 12-year-old retarded boy, producing an 80% suppression of the target behavior. In another clinical trial, Kauffman et al. (1975) imitated the yelping of a 9-year-old trainable retarded girl which stimulated a 50% increase in the yelping. In a conclusion, Kauffman states, "Being imitated may not only be a powerful consequence for some children but may increase cognitive awareness and cognitive control in ways that verbal reminders and instructions do not" (p. 197). He suggests that cognitively primitive children are more responsive to imitation than they are to punishment.

Clinicians in various fields who have experimented with imitation include: Bricker and Bricker (1976) in language training with severely retarded children; Des Lauriers and Carlson (1969) in work with autistic children; and Van Riper (1972) in speech correction.

The rapidly expanding area of imitation has been reviewed by Roberts (1979). His critique examines the three experimental paradigms based on learning theory. While questioning some of the methodology, he points out the complex theoretical issues to be explored in this promising avenue of research.

Using a social cognition approach, Lewis and Brooks–Gunn (1979) have conducted empirical studies of the effect of reflecting self–representations to children ages 9–36 months using mirrors, pictures and videotape representations of these young subjects. Lewis and Brooks–Gunn demonstrate the developmental sequences in the growth of self–representation. Most relevant for the present study is their consistent finding that at all ages tested, the predominant emotional response to a self–reflection was positive as demonstrated by loving, smiling, and laughing.

Spitz (1957) anticipated the above studies. "We may note here that few of us are aware of the fact that it is not only the child who imitates the grownup, but that the obverse is also the case" (p. 41). Decrying the lack of systematic investigation, Spitz declared, "Yet it [being imitated] plays a significant role in the formation and development of object relations both from the viewpoint of the parent and from that of the child" (p. 41).

Anna Freud (1926[1927][a]) described her approach to a 10-year-old boy whose attitude toward her was "of a thoroughgoing rejection and mistrust . . ." Finding that there was no suffering or intrapsychic conflict and the child would not accept her as an ally, Freud approached the boy as follows:

> At first, for a long time, I did nothing but follow his moods along all their paths and bypaths. If he came to his appointment in a cheerful mood, I was cheerful too. If he were serious or depressed, I acted seriously. If he preferred to spend the hour under the table, I would treat it as the most natural thing in the world, lift the tablecloth and speak to him under it. If he came with a string in his pocket, and began to show me remarkable knots and tricks, I would let him see that I could make more complicated knots and do more remarkable tricks. If he made faces, I pulled better ones; and if he challenged me to trials of strength, I showed myself incomparably stronger. But I also followed his lead

> in every subject he talked about, from tales of pirates and questions of geography to stamp collection and love stories. (p. 12)

Aichhorn (1935, 1964) according to published accounts, was probably the first therapist who used mirroring techniques deliberately and with rationale. Noting that delinquents were functioning on a narcissistic level rather than an object level, Aichhorn actively attempted to establish a positive narcissistic transference. He would accomplish this step by *not* aligning himself with society's values, and by candidly presenting himself as being in tune with the delinquent's values. Aichhorn would surprise and "one up" the delinquent, and act like a "glorified replica of the delinquent's ego and ego ideal." Aichhorn tried to manifest approval of the delinquent and tried to get the delinquent to respect and idealize him. When attached to Aichhorn, delinquents would more likely come under not only Aichhorn's control but would develop their own controls through a sense of guilt when they offended Aichhorn. Aichhorn's specialized pioneering approach is more fully discussed by Marshall (1979a, 1979b).

Aichhorn seems to have presaged some of Kohut's concepts in relation to the phenomenon of mirroring in narcissistic states. Kohut (1971) more sharply defines a mirror transference and established it as a central concept in his theory of therapy. But he seldom uses the verb "mirror" because he believes that the mirror transference spontaneously evolves from the empathic understanding attitude of the analyst. He allows that in the treatment of delinquents and some types of gross pathology, the therapist "unavoidably" must actively establish a narcissistic transference. However, at one point he presents all of these as an analytic piece ". . . the listening, perceiving, and echoing-mirroring presence of the analyst now reinforces the psychological forces which maintain the cohesiveness of this self-image . . ." (p. 125). Kohut puts Aichhorn's "special skills" into more modern terms. Aichhorn offered "himself first as a mirror image of the delinquent's grandiose self." For an extended comparison of Aichhorn and Kohut's work, the reader is referred to Marohn (1977).

The client-centered psychotherapy of Carl Rogers (1961) has focused on developing therapists who evolve (a) an empathic understanding of the patient's phenomenological self or internal frame of reference; (b) unconditional positive regard for the patient; (c) a congruence in the relationship—therapists should be fully aware of the response the patient is eliciting in them. Client-centered therapists develop a remarkable sense of reflecting back or paraphrasing the patient's conscious feelings and inner state. The lack of judgmental attitudes and of probing characterize this gentle, sympathetic approach to the patient. Deviations in the therapist's positive view are attended to immediately to restore this positive equilibrium. Rogers advocated no change in the therapist's orientation throughout the treatment. In sum, it appears that from a technical point of view, client-centered therapists engage in considerable mirroring in that they attempt to reflect back to the patient the feeling tone that the patient overtly expresses. Compared to a Kohutian, the client-centered therapist is much more active, attends more to conscious feelings, and has no concept of transference. However, both types of therapists share interesting similarities in regard to the mirroring process.

Stolorow (1976) finds "striking parallels between the techniques, therapeutic processes and ideal outcome" (p. 28) formulated by Kohut and Rogers. He notes that their approaches are particularly well-suited to narcissistic patients who tend to experience any interpretation as a shattering injury to the patient's own grandiose wishful self.

Spotnitz (1976b) grants the process of mirroring a more sophisticated term—"psychological reflection." He contends that there are two forms: echoing and devaluating the object. In the process of echoing schizophrenics who hold themselves in low regard, Spotnitz repeats the patients' self-abnegating expressions. Patients see that the object will remain close to the ego no matter how bad the ego is. Eventually, as the ego gains strength, the patients get tired of the object's reflections and attack it. Spotnitz theorizes that this procedure reverses the original process of ego formation when the infantile mental apparatus failed to release hostile feelings toward its earliest object because the object was too distant. In the process of devaluating the object, Spotnitz interrupts the schizophrenic's self-abnegations by assuming a "me too" position. The patient then feels in a more secure position to attack the therapist and to resolve the idealizing transference.

Related to Spotnitz's orientation is the paradigmatic approach (Nelson, 1968), which makes wide use of mirroring techniques. Strean (1968), in particular, believes that by providing a mirror image of patients, two processes occur: (a) patients find the therapist to be a more interesting person (cf. A. Freud, 1926[1927]a and Aichhorn, 1964); (b) patients eventually more clearly identify themselves and become the objects of analysis (p. 189).

Milton H. Erickson, early in his life, contracted a disease that consigned him to a wheelchair. He subsequently developed phenomenal observational and imitative abilities which he integrated into his therapeutic approach.

> Milton Erickson frequently adopts the client's tonality, syntax and tempo of speech, will adjust his body position, breathing rate and gestures to match the client's. Thus, the client feels his own breathing, the rising and falling of his chest, and simultaneously sees Erickson's body moving with the same rhythmic motions. Erickson extends these principles in every way. He not only matches his breathing to that of the client, but will also match the tempo of his voice to the client's breathing or pulse rate by watching the client's veins expand and contract. He will use words and phrases he has heard the client use and voice inflections used tonally by the client. He, in essence, makes all his own output channels a feedback mechanism that will match his client's subjective exposure on both cs and unc levels. (Bandler and Grinder, 1975, p. 16)

An illustration of Erickson's (1965) mirroring (and satiation) techniques comes from his early work in a hospital where a man with no identification had lived for 6 years. Except for a few words, George talked at length in an incomprehensible language filled with neologisms and word salad. Studying George's language, Erickson improvised and practiced a similar nonsense language. He sat silently with George for increasing amounts of time until a full hour was reached. One day addressing the empty air, Erickson identified himself verbally to which George made no response. On the next day Erickson identified himself directly to George who replied with an "angry stretch of word salad" (p. 501). Erickson replied courteously in his own contrived language, essentially mirroring George. George appeared puzzled, and intoned an incomprehensible question to which Erickson replied in equally incomprehensible terms. After a half dozen interchanges, George became silent and Erickson left. A series of sessions occurred (the number was not specified by Erickson) wherein appropriate greetings were exchanged, George would launch into a long word-salad speech, to which Erickson would reply courteously, and after brief exchanges in their respective languages, George would fall silent and Erickson would resume other activities.

Then, George, after returning the morning greeting, made meaningless utterances without pause for 4 hours. It taxed the author greatly to miss lunch and to make a full reply in kind. George listened attentively and made a two-hour reply to which a weary two-hour response was made. (George was noted to watch the clock throughout the day.)

The next morning George returned the usual greeting properly but added about two sentences of nonsense to which the author replied with a similar length of nonsense. George replied, "Talk sense, Doctor." "Certainly I'll be glad to. What is your name?" "O'Donovan and it's about time somebody who knows how to talk asked. Over 5 years in this lousy joint . . ." (to which was added a sentence or two of word salad). The author replied, "I'm glad to get your name, George. Five years is too long a time . . ." (and about two sentences of word salad were added). (p. 502)

Within a year George was discharged, found a job, and visited Erickson from time to time. Beginning and ending his visits with some word salad, George, at one time, punctuated his session with "nothing like a little nonsense in life, is there, Doctor?"

The 1980 International Congress in Ericksonian Approaches to Hypnosis and Psychotherapy revealed considerable effort spent on understanding why Erickson was successful in his atheoretic therapeutic endeavors. A possible explanation from a psychoanalytic view is that Erickson, in his great capacity to mirror, quickly established intense narcissistic transference. On this emotional foundation, Erickson would issue his directives that tended to be carried out by his patients. Watzlawick (1978) argues that Erickson worked with right brain functions. On this basis, we speculate that mirroring, and perhaps the establishment of the narcissistic transference, is largely a function of the right brain.

E. J. Anthony (1977), in treating a 7-year-old elective mute boy found, "Prior to the emergence of the verbal system in this case, the child and I had begun to mirror each other's movements and to imitate each other's productions. He would sometimes copy a clay figure that I would make and I would do the same" (p. 323).

While not a professional therapist, Kaufman (1976) humanely describes how he mobilized his household into a milieu therapy program for his autistic child. Included in the program was a considerable but unspecified amount of imitation or mirroring of Raun's behavior in the context of an exceptional amount of permissiveness, acceptance, teaching, and physical contact. For example, when Raun spun plates, up to 7 people would be with him spinning plates and pans.

Characteristically, Raun was a gentle loving child who apparently reflected the warm accepting emotional climate. But 24 weeks into the program, he went on a rampage, exuding anger and pushing over furniture, books, papers, etc. His resident teacher–therapist paralleled Raun's frenetic activity. From time to time the child would walk over to his therapist, hug her leg, and then continue his destructive journey. Upon the parents' return 2 days later, a qualitative change had occurred in his verbalizations and relatedness to people.

While it is difficult to discern the part that mirroring played in Raun's development, the report is compatible with the thesis that mirroring is a powerful therapeutic intervention.

Ekstein and Caruth (1971) find echoing to be an important developmental transaction between baby and mother, and a significant therapeutic device in the treatment of psychotic children. "The baby learns the spoken word through echoing and imitating the mother's seeming echo of his inner preverbal sensations and perceptions" (p. 85). Ekstein seems to be talking about a feedback system wherein both mother and child echo each other. Like Winnicott and Piaget, Ekstein finds that the mother's capacity to "feed back" or reflect the baby's inner state, provides an important maturational atmosphere for the child.

> A good mother is not merely a true echo; rather she is what we might call an advanced creative echo—an interpreter—who, like the therapist, makes something new available to the child, for otherwise the infant could never become capable of a true dialogue, for which the recognition of a separate animate object is necessary (p. 85).

In introducing the concept of the mirror, he differentiates it from an echo. "The mirror has more autonomy than the echo; for it has the capacity of reflecting someone other than the self" (p. 85). In citing the case of a schizophrenic boy who could tolerate only an echoing relationship because a mirroring produced a terrorizing threat of his own infantile aggression and sadistic introjects, Ekstein implies that mirroring as opposed to echoing may overwhelm patients with too much information about themselves. Combining echoing and mirroring, Ekstein establishes a therapeutic principle, *". . . to establish contact you must echo, but to develop leverage, you must mirror"* (original italics) (p. 85).

Twin studies, especially by Burlingham (1972), are thought-provoking. "Copying games" between one pair of identical twins, began between 13 and 15 months. Laughter was an essential consequence of the mirroring process. In fact, their mutual excitement led to wild uncontrollable and aggressive movements. Burlingham's impression was that the games did not further the twins' development. This observation coincides with Fouts' (1975) finding that being imitated had differential effects on introversive and extroversive boys, as well as Kauffman et al.'s (1975) work, and some early experiments I conducted with physical mirroring. That is, physical mirroring overstimulated aggression-prone children. However, with deeply inhibited or regressed children, physical mirroring vitalized them. I have abandoned physical mirroring for psychological mirroring. In all likelihood, excessive emotional mirroring may not be in the child's best developmental interests. However, the data strongly suggest that mirroring activates very powerful emotional and physical forces that stem from early stages of development and, as with any therapeutic techniques, must be used with good clinical judgment and dosage.

The research using mirrors and distorted mirrors demonstrates that schizophrenics have body image problems. For example, Orbach et al. (1966) using a mirror whose distortion could be regulated by subjects, found that schizophrenics had great difficulty in creating a distortion-free image of themselves. The subjects had no difficulty in evolving a distortion-free image of a door. In general, the data are consistent with the hypothesis that body image problems develop at an early developmental stage of body-ego differentiation.

There have been psychoanalytic studies of the mirror, the mirror dream, and the mirroring experience. Elkisch (1957), in her report on three psychotic women, found that they used mirrors to protect themselves from a fear of loss of self. Eisnitz (1961) determined that, in mirror dreams, a punitive superego projected onto a mirror can be transformed into a protective superego that is subsequently introjected. Shengold (1974) relates the metaphor of the mirror to the narcissistic stage of development when identity and psychological structures are being formed. Fergelson (1975), in his analysis of mirror dreams, finds that they usually represent narcissistic defenses.

There is an important relationship between projective identification and mirroring. Although projective identification is a complex, ill-defined, and controversial phenomenon, its significance is yet to be fully appreciated. Its development and use has been traced by Ogden (1979) whose three-phase definition is:

> . . . a group of fantasies and accompanying object relations having to do with the ridding of the self of unwanted aspects of the self, the depositing of those unwanted "parts" into another person, and finally with the "recovery" of a modified version of what was extruded. (p. 357)

Ogden also sees projective identification serving the functions of: (a) defense; (b) exerting pressure on the object to think, feel and act as the self; (c) a type of object relatedness wherein the projector experiences the recipient as separate enough to contain the projections, yet similar enough to the self as to warrant a sense of sameness; (d) "a pathway for psychological change," (p. 371) by which the projector reincorporates the projections "processed" by the recipient.

Within this definition, mirroring is viewed as follows. We assume that there is a need for mirroring or, at the very least, that children thrive in an atmosphere of optimal congruence between their feeling state and the way the mother is perceived by them. If that need or convergence is not satisfied, babies, instead of passively resigning themselves to an autistic state, actively struggle to perceive and to generate in the mother those mirroring responses necessary for growth. Though broadly a defense against autism, this process is not viewed as a defense, but as a developmental step and "organizer" analogous to the "No" phenomenon. If children perceive the congruence when, in reality, it is not there, they will probably eventually regress under the weight of reality or possibly maintain their perception as a delusion or quasidelusion. One is reminded of those delinquent and/or borderline children and adolescents who sustain "good" images of their parents in spite of the reality. Also, there are children who criticize their parent(s) but become protective and furious when others join in the criticism.

If the child is successful in inducing congruent behaviors in the other at an optimal rate, the sense of omnipotence and mastery will probably grow, the identification process will be maximized, and the individuation process sustained. If, in the unlikely circumstances the child perceives only convergence, pathology may occur in the form of grandiosity, undifferentiated self–object field, and continued narcissism.

From this shaky theoretic perch, one may venture further out on the limb and reinterpret the myth of Narcissus. The wasting away of Narcissus may be seen as a process engendered by a sterile visual "echoing" wherein Narcissus saw *only* his own image and nothing else. Not only is an echo of the self needed for life, but also a feeding back of a modified self enriched by the object and the outside world—that provided by mirroring and projective identification.

Mirroring not only involves the establishment of a relationship with the narcissistic self (if you are like me, you like me), it also recreates the symbiotic bond that led to the pathology. Thus, a positive or a negative transference may emerge because the patient sees in the therapist those aspects of the mother that damaged the ego or arrested its development. Therefore, the child is also likely to unconsciously feel, "If you are like me and my mother, I am afraid of you because you hate me, want to destroy me, want me to take care of you, are going to abandon me, etc." The ambivalence of the transference is clearly shown in the following case.

Mirroring of the Self and Object

A 12-year-old boy, adopted as an infant, was raised by an angry, emotionally neglectful mother who had been intermittently hospitalized for depression and a father who, although strict and rigid, maintained warmer ties with his son. Referred because of increasing disruptive behavior in school and defiance at home, Jim initially related to me in an idealizing manner as if I were his long-lost parent(s). Soon enough he began to demonstrate the stubbornness, cockiness, contempt, and angry demands for "freedom" that got him into difficulty in school and home. Content of sessions revolved around his attempts to influence me to obtain more independence from his parents and from me through reduced sessions or termination of therapy. I could evoke from him intense complaints about me not caring for him, not wanting him to grow up, and my wanting only to control him and use him to earn money. None of these claims were challenged. In fact, from time to time, I would ask him, "Why should I care for you?" "Why shouldn't I try to control you?" "Why shouldn't I earn money off you?" As his transferential reactions intensified, I could easily discern his playing out with me the role of the angry, neglected child trying to free himself from the bonds of his emotionally needy mother and controlling father. At the same time it seemed that he was trying to work through his feelings about being abandoned by his biological parents. Although I did nothing to dissuade him from his transference feelings, I did maintain a steady interest and regard for his feelings which was a different experience for him. As he gave up his angry complaints and fell into sullen depressed silence, I began to interpret some of his reactions to me. His essential response was the following essay:

> SIDNEY THE GARBAGE CAN
>
> I am a garbage can and nobody cares what happens to me, all people do is fill me with trash. Nobody even stops to take out the time to clean me or even give me a bath. They just leave me there to smell like a skunk and sometimes even worse. In the winter time when it rains and snows they don't even put me in the garage, they let me freeze to death.
>
> One day a miracle happened. I was going to move to Florida but wherever I go they will still probably treat me like the garbage itself. They will probably leave me out in the rain but at least I'm glad there's no snow. But then, one day it happened. A hurricane, fierce one and wouldn't you know they didn't put me in the garage. I was going up in the air it seems I would never land and for my sake I hoped not. But all was not lost I fell in a pool ah! now I really enjoyed it. It was the pool of a wealthy millionaire. He took good care of me, I also had a good time with a shiny gold garbage can and her name was Mary-Ann. We got married and lived in luxury for the rest of our lives.

This suddenly showed what was beneath Jim's angry tirades and accelerating delinquent behavior. He is the empty, worthless, stinking, neglected container to be used for symbiotic needs and projective identifications. Rather than experience these feelings, they were angrily projected onto others. These feelings were probably also part of his mother's split-off emotional life. Under the impact of therapy, he felt he was still being treated like garbage but not as coldly. My ability to take his explosions, and his relief that I did not throw him out or damage him, led him to believe that he was in a safe and secure environment which probably reflected his wishes about his original parents. His increased ego strength and differentiated self also allowed him to become interested in girls, especially one by the name of Mary-Ann.

The relative ease of this case was made possible largely by

setting up the appropriate paradigm dictated by the case material interlocking with the developmental theory. The transference-resistance was predictable, and more importantly, the objective countertransference of wanting to control, use, and abandon this boy was made clear early on and used to advantage.

Being Tutored and Mirroring

A 13-year-old, Denny, was sent for treatment because of his alienation from peers and his highly obnoxious and offensive acting out to friends and family. This very bright boy, in his various efforts to shake me up and get rid of me, hit solidly on teasing, insulting, messing, defying, and otherwise acting in his alienating manner. While I focused on describing his behavior, I also attempted to act in an accepting manner. Denny told me that I would never make a good therapist because I was too pleasant—I wasn't unpleasant enough. I recognized a profound threat and at the same time how offensive he was to me. I asked Denny if he could teach me to be a better therapist—to be more unpleasant. Denny not only agreed to be my mentor, but agreed to write an article entitled "Principles of Being Disagreeable" or "How to be Rotten Without Really Trying." We spent several sessions cataloging "disagreeableness." In general, he would act in his "normal" manner and we would try to derive the principles of disagreeableness such as:

When asked to do something, say "no."
When asked to do something, do the opposite.
Ask impossible questions like, "Who says I am?"
Boast about greatness.
Show no concern at all.

Positive changes in attitude and behavior were reported in school and at home. As I became adept at using the "principles," Denny boasted that he had been a superb teacher and that he had taught his lessons too well, citing, "Always praise yourself" and "Never give credit to the other guy." He told me to stop practicing my unpleasantness, that really he was a very nice fellow and that he had been fooling me all the time. He tried to act in a pleasant manner, but often would fall into his unpleasant ways which permitted him to see the automatic quality of his unpleasantness.

Behavioral change occurred with a minimum surfacing of personal history and current events. Perhaps the change occurred because, as was discovered in the therapy of the parents, Denny's symptoms were produced more by familial conflicts than by intrapsychic disturbance.

This technique, a variation of "mirroring" and "affirmation," consists of getting the patient to teach the therapist the defense-resistance. Denny could begin to give up his defensive maneuvers because he could identify and perceive them more clearly through the therapist, and experience the impact that his maneuvers had on others.

Affirmation, Being Tutored, and Mirroring

Ten-year-old Sue, an identical twin, appeared to be very anxious and distressed about being sent for treatment. After the initial session where she gave very limited information about herself, she settled into responding to all questions with silence, shrugs, "I don't know," "I don't care," etc. Knowing this child suffered a great deal in comparison with her more talented and personable twin, and who was unsure of her own identity, I expressed great delight with her "I don't knows." I proposed that not knowing and not caring about things, people, and feelings at certain times was of very great value. I argued that I was without this ability and that I suffered a great deal because of this deficiency. I gave her the title of "The Queen of the I-Don't-Knowers" and implored her to teach me how to be an "I-don't-knower." She responded with a giggled "I'm not sure" and a shrug of her shoulders. We then embarked upon cataloging all the verbal and nonverbal forms of saying "I don't know." She would answer a variety of questions dealing with her immediate sense perceptions, her memory and her feelings. She was able to indicate time and place of knowing and not knowing. We drew charts of percentages of "I-don't-knows" with various people and conditions. As I began to imitate her and practice my "lessons," she seemed delighted—particularly when I would answer "I don't know" to one of her mother's questions. I was then able to question her identity with her own resistance by saying, "I'm never sure that I see you or your sister." We arranged a secret identity code whereby I would ask, "What is your name?" and she would reply, "I don't know." Finally, when I asked her to what extent she didn't know herself, she indicated that she knew herself "only 20%" and would like to know herself much better. At this point she appeared to be amenable to an exploration of her life.

The affirmation probably worked because the therapist did not display the usual response to her indecision, turning away, and underproductivity. Her parents, overtly, had been offended by the girl's detachment. On a deeper level, Sue "knew" many things that she did not want to face and was not sure anyone could understand or care. The affirmation of her defense reassured her that the therapist would not force her to reveal her experiences prematurely and the mirroring helped her see more clearly her stimulus-value and impact on others. By putting her in the position of the tutor, the therapist clearly indicated that he wanted to be like her—and that he liked her. Whenever exploration of herself faltered we would fairly easily gain our pace by playing a card game of "I don't know" that we had created.

Research on Joining

To date there appear to be only two direct attempts to study the phenomenon of joining experimentally. Basing his approach on Freud's attempt to verify hypotheses, Brandt (1974) discussed evolving means of testing hypotheses about his own interventions in a clinical situation. His joining of patients seemed to induce clinically significant material. Meadow (1974), in a more controlled clinical experiment, demonstrated that mirroring as compared with interpretative interventions induced "greater depth of feeling, and with more related history and insight into their defenses" (p. 92).

Indirect evidence about the effect of joining is apparent in Marshall's (1958) study of self-concept. Using stimulated peer appraisals of saliant self-variables such as honesty and fairness,

Marshall found that subjects significantly lowered their self-esteem when negatively appraised. Relative to control conditions, subjects did not raise their self-esteem under positive conditions. The control group, which received appraisals congruent with their self-concept, was not significantly different from the praised group. The experiment clearly demonstrated that negative peer pressure is more likely to change self-concept than positive peer pressure. However, the fact that the positive and congruent peer appraisals produced similar results commands further study.

Further Definitions

All of the above techniques—affirmation, ordering, suggesting, satiation, consultation, countermanding parental resistance, mirroring, and being tutored—appear to have several factors in common:

The therapist silently identifies the resistance.

The therapist communicates in a deliberate manner consistent with the dynamics that he or she understands that the resistance is an extremely valuable aspect of the patient's character structure.

The therapist communicates that the continued operation of defense-resistance is necessary for the continued functioning of the individual and that the defense-resistance will be accepted and even supported—not attacked or broken—until the person has the awareness and ego strength to replace it with a more adaptive and controlled behavior pattern. Resistance joining is a technique of therapeutic response to resistances that preserves the defense, makes it less automatic (puts it more within the control of the ego), and promotes further self-understanding.

Provisions for the Use of Joining Techniques

To determine the appropriate technique to be used, it is essential to know the dynamics of the family. If, as in the cases of Lidz, Fleck, and Cornelison (1965), the children's symptoms literally hold the families in balance, no technique for symptom reduction or change is called for until the therapist can predict the result of an intervention.

Another provision in the use of joining techniques with children and adolescents is that the parents be in counseling. Sometimes, the techniques overshoot their mark. Symptoms may disappear too quickly and parents may withdraw the child from treatment prematurely. Also, the child may give a bizarre account of the therapist's efforts thereby endangering further involvement.

Joining techniques may be used when the child is obviously threatened or extremely anxious in the treatment situation. They are also effective where there is no verbalized anxiety in the presence of massive repression or psychotic defenses such as projection, denial, or splitting. Joining techniques can be used when resistance to treatment becomes manifest and usual techniques appear to have no impact. Joining techniques are probably more appropriately used with certain kinds of disorders. As suggested by Spotnitz (1969) and Slavson (1970) joining techniques may be employed with the narcissistic disorders for which traditional psychoanalytic techniques have not been proven as they have with neurotic disorders.

The choice of joining techniques may be *suggested* by the countertransference and induced countertransference feelings of the therapist. For example, induced feelings of helplessness may suggest acting in a helpless manner or a strong authoritative way. Before joining techniques are employed, the therapist must be able to predict the impact on the patient with a high degree of probability. The techniques are *not* designed for inexperienced, untrained, or "wild" therapists who pride themselves on being atheoretic. They are designed to be used by therapists who have been well-analyzed and who are acquainted with their residual pathology and characterological styles.

Maenchen (1970) indicates that " 'playing' the defenses" and role playing (p. 191) are not suitable in child analysis because they provide too much gratification for the child. While this principle appears to be valid for the treatment of neurotic children, one wonders about its validity for preoedipal children. However, there is an implicit danger in the overuse of joining techniques: the techniques may overstimulate or overactivate certain trauma that produces excessive regressive, agitated, or acting-out behavior. At these signs, the therapist must desist and change strategy. Harley (1970) also warns therapists that in their zealousness to establish rapport, they do not side with the negativism and hostility of adolescence that instigate acting-out.

The therapist must watch for an increase in acting-out due to the child making the mistake in assuming that "if it's O.K. to talk about it, it's O.K. to do it." Therefore, in general, the therapist must constantly differentiate talking from acting and, in particular, differentiate between behavior in the sessions and behavior in school or at home. The child must be impressed with the fact that the therapy sessions are very special occasions, different from any others. Children should come to know that they are allowed and supposed to say everything on their minds during the session, but that this principle must be used with considerable discretion outside therapy. The therapist should always keep in mind that catharsis or "acting on" strivings is not the goal of therapy—the first aim is the resolution of resistances to talking about everything.

Finally, the use of joining techniques is not an end in itself, but is a means of furthering the total treatment process. It does not produce "a cure," but does facilitate resolution of defense-resistances that sets the stage for personality change.

Chapter 4

THE RATIONALES AND PARALLELS

PSYCHOANALYSIS

The rationale for employing joining techniques, especially in the treatment of narcissistic, borderline, and preoedipal conditions, is relevant in Freud's discussions and treatment of resistance. While recognizing that resistances provided the analyst a window on the patient's earlier life and clues to the development of symptoms and defenses, he implied that the analyst give patients time to reactivate, mobilize, and to unfold their resistance, particularly the crucial transference resistance. When addressing himself to the therapeutic problems presented by the psychotic and those with weak egos, Freud advocated strengthening of the ego before interpretative activity. We cannot forget Freud's (1940[1938]a) counsel that the vulnerable ego "must be constantly encouraged and soothed if it is not to fail us" (p. 178). His orientation toward the treatment of children was clearly that "analytic influence must be combined with educational measures" (p. 215) and that "something other than analysis must be employed, though something which will be at one with analysis in its *purpose*" (p. 274).

Child Psychoanalysis

As indicated in the first chapter, Anna Freud and other child analysts advocate "truly analytic measures" for the neurotic child whose conflicts are primarily intrapsychic and whose ego is intact and age-appropriate. Interpretative activity decreases as a function of the weakness of the ego while educational ego-strengthening efforts are generally recommended.

Some parallels can be drawn between the treatment approaches to the preoedipal adult and the child. In general, the listening, accepting, mirroring position of the analyst as typified by Kohut provides a model in contrast to the highly interpretative and confrontational approach of Kernberg, Masterson, and Rinsley.

Behavior Therapy

A great common ground that psychoanalytically oriented therapy has with behavior therapy is that both endeavor to evoke or allow the emergence of anxiety-producing thoughts, feelings, and memories of the patient in the context of understanding, acceptance, and counteranxiety cues. Behavior therapy relies more on principles and techniques, while analytic therapy emphasizes the emotional relationships between patient and therapist.

Several behavioral techniques seem to have a similarity to joining techniques, noninterpretative approaches to resistances and symptoms, and also to those therapies that try to induce a "corrective emotional experience." A. Wolberg (1973) parallels Ferenczi's "active therapy" with behavior therapy (p. 186). Wachtel (1973) provides a more extended contrast of behavior therapy with psychoanalysis.

Systematic Desensitization

This process is based on the principle of reciprocal inhibition or counterconditioning in which an anxiety or "maladaptive" response is elicited from the patient and is paired with and inhibited by an incompatible response that is usually positive and rewarding. Relaxation exercises according to modifications of Jacobson's technique create the positive condition. A hierarchy of difficult situations are evolved. Imagining the least anxiety-arousing situation in the state of relaxation, the patient proceeds down the hierarchy until anxiety is experienced. Relaxation is again induced and the process is repeated. Clinicians such as Wachtel (1973) and Paul (1966) maintain that the principles that account for anxiety reduction with systematic densensitization are the same ones that operate in more traditional therapies.

Implosive Therapy

This behavioral approach is an extension of some of the principles used in desensitization. The process is as follows: the therapist elicits those events, feelings, memories, thoughts, or fantasies from the patient that evoke avoidance, anxiety, or other unwanted reactions. After a relevant history of the symptoms is obtained, the patient is trained to imagine the disturbing complex. In the implosive sessions themselves, the therapist directs imaginal scenes which include the aversive situation. According to Stampfl (1976), the therapist actively, persistently and directly expands the imagery trying to recreate the conditions and affective reactions attendant to the trauma.

Stimulus Satiation

In two studies, behavior therapists have used "stimulus satiation" to diminish undesirable behavior. Welsh (1971) reports two cases of juvenile firesetters who, in the course of their therapy, were "forced" to light matches under certain rules. Initially, the children were delighted with the directives, but after three and seven satiation sessions were conducted respectively, the children protested and pleaded to do other things. A dramatic termination of their firesetting outside of the therapy room was reported.

Ayllon (1963), after establishing the cooperation of the nursing staff, treated a towelhoarding hospitalized schizophrenic by supplying the patient with so many towels that they overflowed the patient's room. This approach is similar to "prescribing the symptom."

Learning Theory

Miller (1959, pp. 205–206) provides a number of postulates or assumptions derived from animal studies from which he deduces hypotheses that, in turn, have been tested for verification. These postulates are cast into psychoanalytic terms for the purposes of this book.

"The tendency to approach a goal is stronger the nearer the subject is to it. This is an application of Hull's principle of the goal gradient and will be called the Gradient of Approach." In psychoanalytic terms, the strength of a drive (impulse) is a function of the nearness to its satisfaction and will be called "Gradient of Drive" illustrated in Figures 4–1, 2, 3. The term "goal," for purposes of this analysis, denotes the emergence into consciousness of a defended against thought, feeling, memory, or wish.

"The tendency to avoid a feared stimulus is stronger the nearer the subject is to it. This was an extension of the general idea of the gradient of reinforcement to avoidance learning. It will be called the Gradient of Avoidance." In psychoanalytic terms, the strength of a defense-resistance is a function of the nearness a person is to a feared or anxiety-producing object and will be called "Gradient of Defense-Resistance" illustrated in the figures.

"The strength of avoidance increases more rapidly with nearness than does that of approach. In other words, the gradient of avoidance is steeper than that of approach. This was a new assumption necessary to account for the behavior of going part way and then stopping." In psychoanalytic terms, the strength of the defense-resistance *increases* more rapidly than the drive as the person nears the conflict object. Also, the strength of the defense-resistance *decreases* more rapidly than the drive as the person moves away from the conflict object. Note that the Gradient of Defense-Resistance is steeper than the Gradient of Drive.

This assumption accounts for the fact that in a conflict situation the patient (a) does not, by definition, reach the goal; (b) when far enough from the goal, proceeds toward it.

"The strength of tendencies to approach or avoid varies directly with the strength of the drive upon which they are based. In other words, an increase in drive raises the *height* of the entire gradient. This assumption was necessary to explain the fact that stronger shocks stopped the animals whereas weaker shocks did not and also to explain the intuitively expected result that stronger shocks would be necessary to stop hungrier animals. This assumption was a specific application of the general notion that response strength varies with relevant drive."

In psychoanalytic terms, the drives and defense-resistances vary in strength. Specifically, when patients are highly motivated, they will move closer to their goal, but at a cost of threat to the defense-resistance which is anxiety.

"Below the asymptote of learning, increasing the number of reinforced trials will increase the strength of the response tendency that is reinforced." In psychoanalytic terms, the therapist can increase the strengths of the drives by encouragement, pointing out success, etc. The therapist can strengthen defense-resistances by support or joining.

"When two incompatible responses are in conflict, the stronger one will occur." In psychoanalytic terms, when drives and defense-resistances are in conflict, the stronger one will occur. This is a reflection of the dynamic principle of psychoanalysis.

The following analysis is based on Miller's expositions (1959,1966). Certain statements can be deduced from the assumptions above.

When patients approach a goal, they stop because of the anxiety induced. As long as the defense-resistance gradient is lower than that of the drive, patients can proceed toward their goals with tolerable anxiety. As they approach their goals and the gradient of drive becomes lower than the defense-resistance gradient, anxiety becomes greater than the motivation for cure so patients retreat to the region of the intersection of the gradients. Operating on the goal side of the intersection increases anxiety and produces stronger defense-resistances, including leaving therapy (Figure 4–1).

Figure 4–2 shows that raising the height of the drive gradient from Y to X (increasing strength of drive) should move the conflict point near to the feared goal and raise the anxiety level from

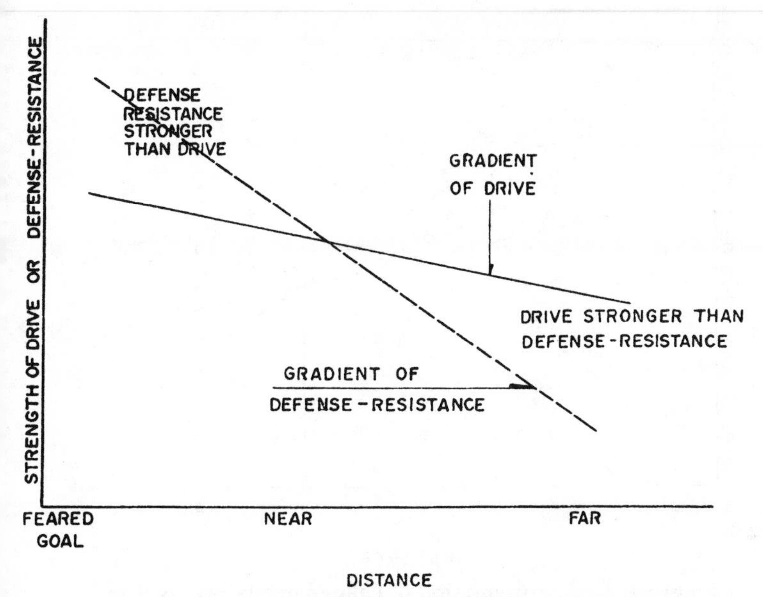

Figure 4–1 Simple graphic representation of a conflict. The drive is stronger far from the feared goal whereas the defense-resistance is stronger near the goal. When far from the goal, the person will approach the goal and stop. When near the goal, he will move away from the goal. He will tend to operate in the region where the gradients cross. It should be noted that the gradients are represented by straight lines in the diagrams. It is likely that the gradients are really complex curves, but which still hold the properties described in this schema.

The feared goal is defined as a thought, affect, or memory which is not within the awareness of the person (unconscious). Nearness and farness from the feared goal are entirely subjective constructs of the person, which the therapist must understand.

Y to X. This can be accomplished in therapy by the conscious or unconscious approval of or encouragement by the therapist to achieve an insight, experience affect, or reach an external goal. For example, a therapist may make an interpretation or indicate

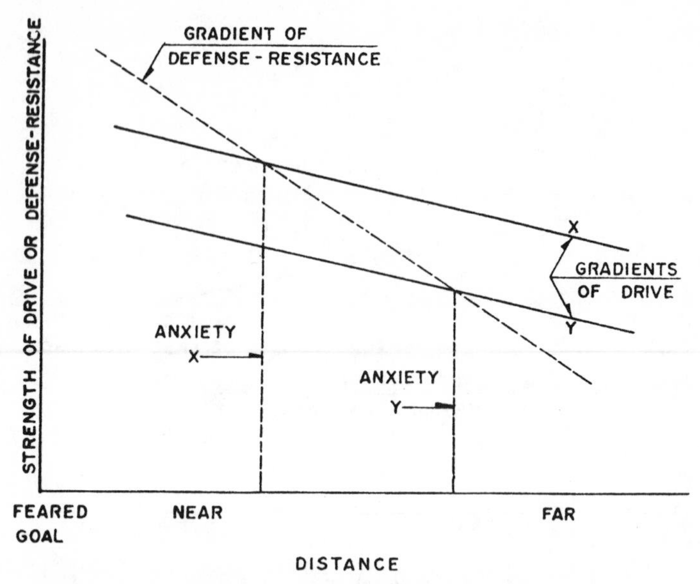

Figure 4–2 Representation of change in anxiety level as a function of change in drive with defense-resistance held constant.

impatience with therapeutic progress. Or the therapist may compliment the patient for progress with implied request for more. Of course, drive can be increased by external factors such as self-motivation and pressure of significant persons. Assuming that a therapist can increase the drive toward the goal, a second deduction is: as the patient moves toward the goal, and holding the defense-resistance constant, anxiety should increase. This deduction is apparent from Figure 4–2 where anxiety Y increases in strength to anxiety X.

A third deduction is possible: holding drive constant, an increase in defense-resistance *reduces* the level of anxiety.

It is this final deduction upon which the rationale rests for supporting, strengthening, or joining defense-resistances. True, this process moves the patient further from the goal, but the reduction of a patient's anxiety and reduction of negative affect in the therapist may provide enough strength for both to proceed in an easier manner. (Figure 4–3)

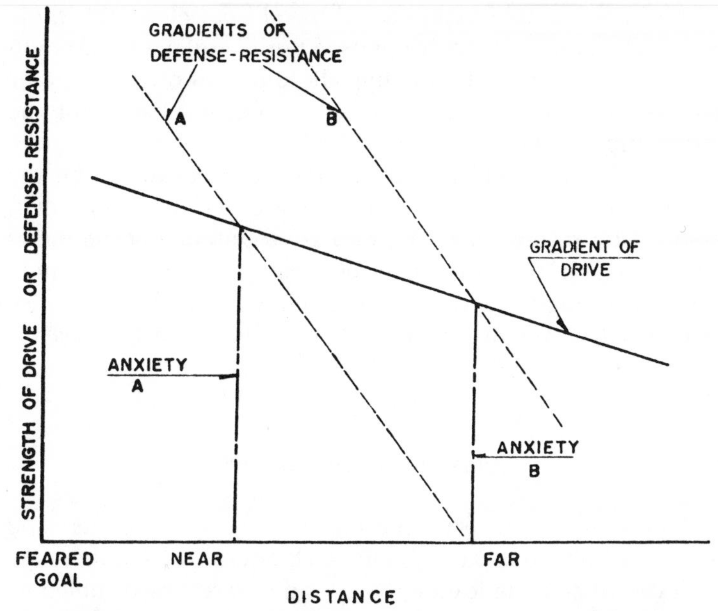

Figure 4–3 Representation of change in anxiety level as a function of changes in defense-resistance with drive held constant.

Miller (1966) has already observed that lowering the gradient of avoidance, rather than raising the gradient of approach, is a more desirable method.

"I believe that this is the reason why in dealing with severe conflicts, it usually is best to concentrate first on reducing the fear motivating the avoidance rather than to try to increase the drives motivating approach. Psychoanalysts describe this strategy as analyzing the resistance" (p. 4).

As can be seen from the graphs, much less anxiety is induced per unit of approach to the goal by lowering the resistances. Also, the "chaotic situation" produced by wild interpretations can be readily seen from the graphs.

Another deduction is that a lowering of the drive decreases the amount of anxiety. Joining techniques tend to lower the motivation to reach the goal of experiencing a particular thought, affect, or memory, or in achieving any goal when the patient is resistive. For example, in the case of David (see below), the whole idea of talking was explicitly opposed until enough ego strength was generated. And certainly the whole notion of reflecting or mirroring relieves the patient of any need for change for the therapeutic moment.

Therefore, the efficacy of joining techniques rests on the principle of reducing anxiety. This goal is especially important in persons with severe disorders, who are frightened of the therapeutic situation, or both. When the anxiety level is low enough, when ego strength is strengthened, and when anxiety tolerance is enhanced, then more traditional methods and techniques can be applied.

COMMUNICATION THEORY

The double-bind principle may be invoked to understand some of the phenomena of joining techniques. Briefly, there are two levels of communication, overt and covert, which sometime correspond to verbal and nonverbal levels of communication. In a disparity between the overt and covert message, the receiver is thrown into conflict. The theory of the "superego lacunae" may be introduced here to emphasize that the covert message given by the parent(s) to children is usually an unconscious command to function pathologically in order to satisfy the unconscious wishes of the parent(s). Yet when children overtly carry out the covert command, they are punished or "scapegoated." The two other conditions for the operation of the double-bind are: the victim cannot leave the "field," and no discussion of the conditions or operations is permitted.

When children display symptoms such as cheating, lying, or silence, they may be carrying out the covert unconscious wishes of the parent. When the therapist joins the symptom expressed in the resistance, children are at first surprised and bewildered because the therapist's valuation is not the usual response to their behavior. After the startled and puzzled stage, tension reduction usually occurs in the form of a deep sigh, and frequently smiling, laughter, or an increased interest in the therapist. Children are pleased to have their emotional cake and eat it too. For if they initially assume that the therapist holds the same covert dictate as the parent, but finds that the therapist does not send the same overt message, they are relieved of the conflict between overt and covert messages. For example, in the case of the Cheater (see below), John was identified with his father's covert wish for him to cheat, be shrewd etc. When I joined his cheating behavior, John's tension level dropped considerably. Even when children finally see that the therapist has a different covert message, they can be loyal to the parent(s), act out their unconscious wishes and not be punished—in fact, be lauded. The double bind is therefore broken, the conflict dispelled, and the tension relieved at two levels. Children will see the therapist as one who will not throw them into conflict and they are grateful to be in the therapist's presence. One might argue that the therapist is supporting and reinforcing pathological behavior. From a naive behavioral point of view, the answer is "yes." But empirically, increase in pathological behavior rarely occurs. Rather, the opposite occurs. The old patterns are broken up and if there is any strength or drive for self-actualization within the child, he or she will gravitate toward healthier behavior. Moreover, the child readily reads the covert message of the therapist, which is "Tell me the story of your life so that you will know yourself and mature." The child, therefore, is temporarily placed in another kind of double bind with the therapist because the overt message is "It's O.K. to be your defensive self." What does the child do in this quandry and metaconflict? The therapist is creating a double bind opposite to that required by the parents. The therapist covertly says "Grow up" and overtly says "It's O.K. to be infantile." At this point, the more pathological child tends to gravitate toward the parental decree while the healthier child will choose the therapist's direction.

The child is, in effect, faced with a "therapeutic paradox" discussed by communication therapists such as Haley (1963) and Watzlawick (1978). Moreover, the negativistic child tends to fight against the therapist's overt message to maintain defenses, especially in the application of satiation and ordering. Children with some ego strength and a reasonable alliance with the therapist become aware of the inappropriateness of their defense-resistance and follow the covert message of the therapist which, in the course of treatment, is made increasingly overt by the therapist.

Chapter 5

THE RESOLUTION OF RESISTANCES OF CERTAIN CHARACTER TYPES
A Form of Character Analysis

Certain behaviors manifested by children in treatment tend to induce nonconstructive countertransference reactions in therapists. These behaviors may reflect major characterological defenses and resistances, but may also represent temporary stages in treatment. If not seen in correct perspective, and if not handled appropriately, treatment may be lengthened, incomplete, or terminated prematurely.

This chapter describes typical troublesome resistance patterns that distress therapists and provides clinical anecdotes illustrating means of handling these patterns with "joining techniques." These techniques tend to go along with, support, or actively strengthen defense-resistances in the interest of reducing anxiety and strengthening the ego. Only upon this base of strength can the ego and character be analyzed.

Formulating the Treatment Plan

A question to the patient that frequently enlightens the therapeutic approach is "How can I help you?" Usually, the reply is a startled "I don't know" or an answer implying "You're the doctor." The therapist's reply is something like "Tell me all about yourself, tell me the story of your life, or tell me anything that comes into your mind." Frequently, the next association or so is a crucial one.

P: I don't know why I think of this now, but I'm reminded of our old house in the country we just bought. When we bought it, the main floor beam of the house was sagging. My father and I put jacks under the beam to straighten it.
T: How did the jacks work?
P: Well, we put three jacks under the beam and you had to be very careful about turning the screw.
T: How's that?
P: If you turned the screw too rapidly the beam might crack and the whole house would tumble down. We had to turn the jacks a little bit each week.
T: How long will it take?
P: I'm not sure.
T: Take a guess.
P: About two years.

In this brief encounter, a 12-year-old unconsciously communicated his feelings of vulnerability and his request that we work slowly. He also was revealing to me his concern about the mutual latent homosexual feelings between himself and his father and delineated the nature of the transference to be. Moreover, his estimate of two years proved to be a fairly accurate guess of the length of treatment.

A Shrugger

Jeff, a 9-year-old, was referred because of uncommunicativeness, passive–aggressive babyish behavior, and unwillingness to work at school. Conceived before his parents' marriage, he was treated in an indifferent, almost neglectful manner by his mother, but was cared for by a mild, more sensitive father.

In his initial session, Jeff responded to my questions with "I don't know" or "I forget" along with corresponding grunts and head and shoulder movements. I indicated that he apparently had great talent in not knowing anything, or, when he did learn something, he could forget it. I asked him if he would be willing to help me with a problem. He answered with a shrug of the shoulders and a quizzical look.

I told him that in my head was a terrible jumble that I wanted to get rid of, and that if I could avoid learning so many facts or could forget the jumbled facts, I would be very appreciative. I also told him I was going on a vacation in 4 weeks and it was necessary to work on the problem now so that I could enjoy the vacation. I added that perhaps he could help me to avoid people coming to me for problems outside my practice. I entreated him to help me evolve "Rules For Not Knowing." His first response was "I don't know if I can help you." I used this response as the basis for the first rule, "When somebody asks for help, say 'I don't know if I can help you.' " I affirmed the validity of his statement by indicating that as a therapist I often got into trouble because I did not always adhere to that rule. When I asked him a few more questions, he answered with his typical, "I don't know," shrug of shoulders, or silence. I listed each of his responses as valid rules of "not knowing." Over the next couple of sessions we evolved more rules, largely by my asking questions, observing the response, and describing it in words. Some of the rules emerged as follows: yawn; look at your watch a lot; think of or wish you were someplace else; be restless; make it look as though you're not interested; doodle; sing to yourself; doze off. In the process I would praise his contribution and explain how each of these rules could be helpful to me in preventing any learning about a person. He seemed very amused and became more talkative when I asked him for and received permission to practice the rules with him.

When I returned from my vacation, I thanked him for his direction and rules saying that they proved helpful in getting rid of the jumble in my head and preventing further jumble. I noted that not caring and not getting involved with people seemed to be the key to avoiding confusion.

I asked him about his summer and about what we should do

with the hour; he resorted to his response of indifference. After some silence, he ambled around the room. I asked him if he would mind if I did something. With his permission, I began a game of solitaire. In response to my questions, Jeff indicted that he knew nothing about the game. However, as I "neglected" him and became involved in my game, Jeff came closer, began telling me about possible moves, and making moves for me. As I kept focused on the game, he began telling me about a new car the family bought. Whenever I showed any interest in his words, he tended to become quiet. In subsequent sessions, we played games requiring verbalizations but that remained in the realm of fantasy or did not require personal disclosures or obvious mutual relatedness.

The therapeutic strategy emerged from knowing that Jeff had been rejected by his mother and from my induced countertransference experience of being rejected by Jeff. Jeff was identifying with the rejecting mother and avoiding a situation where he could be rejected. My overt position of affirming his not wanting to become involved was designed to show Jeff that I was not about to be put off by his defense, nor would I violate it, but in fact value it and retain it for myself. My overt "neglect" with covert caring recreated for him the original traumatic situation, but cast in a manner that he could manage.

A Detached and Indifferent Child
("The nonengaging child"–Neubauer [1976])

A resistant 10-year-old, in spite of his protestations and open dislike of therapy, progressed rapidly in his heretofore deteriorating school situation, after I explained to him that I wanted to learn how to be as detached and indifferent as he. We evolved this list over several sessions.

How to be an "I-don't-knower"

Say

I don't know

Sometimes

It doesn't matter

I guess so
I think
That's about it
I don't care
I don't mind
Who, me?
I forget
Yes
No
Pretty good
It's all the same to me
Sort of
I don't remember
Maybe yes, maybe no
It doesn't make any difference

This boy was both enraged and fascinated by my approach which allowed him to work through the pain and humiliation he had suffered in a school that not only did not recognize a serious learning disability, but had communicated that "he could do better if he wanted." In the therapeutic situation, he found that he could exercise and be rewarded for all the defensive maneuvers that he had evolved in coping with an impossibly demanding school situation. As the stresses of school diminished, we were able to explore how he had used the similar defenses to cope with the demands of an obsessive–compulsive father and an overprotective mother from whom he was trying to individuate.

A Silent Child

Ten-year-old David was referred because of negativistic, excited, and destructive behavior at home and anxious, noncommunicative behavior in school. Basically, no verbalization of feeling was permitted at home.

In the first 6 months of treatment, David made adequate progress in that he was able to talk to a degree about his family and school situation. However, as he came to the task of discussing relevant feelings, he became quite uncommunicative and wanted only to build toy models for a long time. One day he brought his report card in. While most teachers pointed out his limited verbal productivity, one teacher's comment was that David essentially had no control over his talking. He saw the latter as a problem and agreed to work on it with me. As the first step, I indicated that he should not talk at all in the sessions. He became very lively, asking me many questions, objecting, and complaining. I explained to him that by learning and practicing control with me, he could control himself better in school. I did grant him the privilege of writing on the blackboard and indicated that I might write back or talk. The sessions consisted of each of us building our respective models until frustration would build up and he would write on the blackboard. Finally, he indicated that he wanted to talk. When I asked him why he wanted to talk, he became very puzzled and could not come up with an answer. I told him that I found it more comfortable not to talk. At this point he "discovered" the puppets and he acted and talked out many of the family conflicts. This experience provided a breakthrough, for he then clearly asked for time to talk, giving appropriate reasons. Initially, we agreed to devote only a portion of our time to talking. This approach is similar to the "learning for spite" by Kesten (1955).

The therapeutic strategy was based on the frustrating silence of the sessions and the awareness that the parents prohibited verbal emotional communication. When I "ordered" him to use his defense-resistance of silence and "mirrored" him in my own silence, he seemed to fight against using his resistance and to reassure himself that I meant to respect his defense.

A Rose-Colored-Glass Child

Cora was an isolated 9-year-old who was extremely dominating through direct demands, fearful whining, wheedling, and clinging. There was a large element of underlying guilt, anxiety, and depression related to her being an adopted child and to the fact that she had been separated from her mother for 4 weeks when she was 11 months old. The major dynamic problem was that of mother–child symbiosis.

Afraid to talk because she felt a danger to the symbiosis, that I would find out that she was defective, and would confront her with her warded-off feelings, Cora maintained a superficial, charming chit-chat that was half fantasy and half reality. She disparaged any attempt I made to contact her emotionally. She presented herself, her family, and friends in a pleasant, favorable light. As she spoke more positively about how well her life was going and how much fun she was having, I felt she was getting further away from her real feelings by redoubling her defensive effort. I told her that of all the children I ever knew, she was the one who seemed to have the most fun. She seemed very pleased with the comment and burst out laughing when I asked her if I could call her the "Princess of Fun and Games." I said in essence, "You have fun in situations where children I see are unhappy. Would you be willing to help me by explaining to me how you go about having fun so that maybe I can tell other children how they can have fun?" When she agreed eagerly, I suggested that she only talk about "fun things" and I would make a list called "How to Have Fun." She began to enumerate: find houses where children live and visit them with your mother; invite a child to your house, ask her what she likes to play, take turns in giving ideas about playing; join the Girl Scouts; and so on. For several weeks I listed about 30 activities that were "fun." During this time she told me a great deal about her life, although not in a very deliberate and integrated manner. As she began to run out of items she said, "I'm tired of telling you only good things. Do you know what bad things happen too?" Reflecting her own caution and in context of our agreement I suggested making a list of things that could make children unhappy. And off we were to the world of feeling that she had kept hidden from me and herself.

Her mother, who was in counseling with me, reported at this time a considerable positive change in Cora's attitude and behavior toward friends and school that suggested a diminution of the symbiotic tie. In counseling the mother, I generally directed her to challenge rather than encourage Cora's independent moves.

As Cora was assured that her mother wanted to maintain the symbiosis, she was able to move away from her. At one point, when it became evident to the mother that Cora was separating from her, she developed a stomach disorder diagnosed as a "latent ulcer." As I became increasingly important to Cora and to her mother, the individuation process progressed more smoothly.

Becoming increasingly aware of being shut out of Cora's life and experiencing dysphoria about the situation, I was able to connect my feelings with Cora's early separation and her desperate need to maintain the symbiotic tie with the mother. I therefore participated in and affirmed her defense-resistance in order to strengthen it until she felt secure enough to deal with underlying distress.

A Mistrustful Adolescent

Sam was the 14-year-old son of an upper-middle-class family and was referred for shoplifting, underachievement, and irresponsible behavior. He came to treatment only because it was a condition of his parole. He barraged me with resistant behavior ranging from denial that he had done anything to a refusal to answer questions. He simply felt that he did not belong in my office, but soon realized he was stuck with me until the court lifted the order. He indicated that all he wanted from me was a report to his parole officer that he kept his appointments. I asked him if he would be willing to sit in the waiting room during his appointment time. He said he did not like the idea because he might be seen there by other people. He did agree to sit in my office by himself. I then asked him if I could see another patient in another room during his time. He asked me if I would expect to get paid. When I said, "Absolutely," he woke up and scolded me because I was a cheat, a crook, a liar. When I asked him what was wrong with my being a cheat, a crook, a liar, he launched into a moralistic tirade ending with, "I can't trust you!"

T: Why should you trust me?

P: If you're a therapist you should be trustworthy.

T: What's wrong with my being untrustworthy with you?
P: Well, some day I may have a problem and want to discuss it.

He insisted that I be present and outlined how I should conduct myself. He became more and more interested in me and himself and treatment progressed in a satisfactory manner.

My role in the above encounter was a direct mirroring or reflection of Sam's behavior. Struck with the similarity between myself and him, he probably sensed that I would do nothing prematurely to violate his need to mistrust others.

A Rule-Changer and Cheater

A 9-year-old borderline boy, suffering from enuresis, encopresis, and marked school underachievement had been the first born. He felt cheated by his mother each time another of three children was born. His father was a management consultant and was well-known as a forceful and shrewd negotiator. He tended to ignore his child while harshly expecting model behavior.

After revealing his psychotic fantasies, John balked at further sessions and would come only if he could play games. In all games, he was extremely competitive and when not winning, he would change the rules in order to gain his advantage. As my frustration and annoyance mounted, I tended to confront him with the nature of his behavior, which he denied. Considering his underlying rage and fear of loss of control as well as his dynamics, I told him that his rule changes kept me on my toes, made the games more interesting, and that he was "The King of the Rule-Makers." He appeared very pleased but changed and widened his attempts at winning. He demonstrated many modes of cheating, swindling, and manipulating. Again, rather than harshly confronting him with his maneuvers, I told him that I admired his capacity to win—no matter how. He countered with, "Yeh, nice guys come in last!" which was a beautiful condensation of his philosophy of life. I indicated that I too liked to win and asked him if he would be kind enough to teach me all of his devices for being first. He agreed with the proviso that I not use his devices against him except in real games. We spent many weeks playing different games wherein he would try to win, and would extract and catalog "John's Rules of Winning." Some examples of his rules were:

> If you are losing—extend game.
>
> Stop game when winning—when winning and other guy comes in strong, end game.
>
> Snicker when other guy is having a hard time.
>
> Insist on going first.
>
> When other person is doing well—interfere with his play: (a) distract him (b) spoiling his score.
>
> Take whatever advantage comes your way and play dumb when confronted.
>
> When adding up score, make mistakes in your favor.
>
> When keeping score, make columns sloppy and not straight so that errors can be easily made in your favor.
>
> When counting for a turn, start with total score and add points from that turn.
>
> Use the highest total score for your own.
>
> When you are winning, change rules to make scoring more difficult.
>
> Immediately put other person at disadvantage—so he has a harder time.
>
> Go first.
>
> Try to control other person.
>
> Pay no attention to the other person's complaint about his disadvantage.
>
> When other guy scores, act as if he didn't and don't add it in.
>
> Try to take over other person's score.
>
> When challenged, tell the other person that he is crazy.
>
> Keep insisting you're right.
>
> Change rules of scoring to your advantage, especially when no stated agreement has been made.

Pay no attention to the other guy when it's his turn and enjoy playing something else.

Go first and if your score is poor, claim that it was just warm-up or practice and it doesn't count.

Be the counter of scores—count up the other guy's score wrong (less).

When other guy complains—criticize him.

When he objects too much—threaten him—kill him.

Always carry a gun.

Always try to be in a more powerful position than the other guy.

When the other guy objects, distract him with something interesting.

When the other guy retaliates, start all over and put yourself in a position so that he can't harm your game.

Make up new rules on the spot to benefit yourself and when the other guy objects (bugging) say "you can do it too."

When you are winning, drive the other guy out of the game by bugging him and not stopping.

When other guy objects, strong arm him.

When you are winning, break the game (break up the game) so that the game can't continue.

Scare the other guy.

Call times when the other guy is doing good and you are not in control.

In a new game, make no mention of rules, but make up rules as you go along to your advantage.

When playing, treat the other player as if he is your slave.

When the other guy seems to have the advantage—shoot 'em down.

Arrange things so that if your opponent makes a score, he damages something he values.

When losing, reverse the score and claim a reversal of rules having to do with scoring.

When losing, get the other guy's interest to play another game.

Cheat or take obvious unfair advantage and then, when the other player objects, talk with him as if it was nothing.

Always deny cheating.

If you can't beat them, join them.

After 3 months of the above activity, he was able to discuss the competitive situation in his family and to reveal his murderous rage at not being "number one." In the meantime, symptoms abated and school work improved. Blocked, frustrated, and enraged at John's behavior, I was able to appreciate his own underlying feelings about the inaccessibility of both parents. Essentially conducting myself in a manner that was the reverse of my initial feelings, I joined him rather than trying to beat him as I began to marvel at his machinations. I stopped attacking his defensive maneuvers and valued them to the point of asking him to tutor me in his defense.

A Thrower

A 6-year-old autistic, unmanageable boy who was virtually nonverbal, spent his sessions throwing toys and dolls, usually into wastebaskets and out of windows. In this activity, he was recreating the many times he had been hospitalized for multiple diseases throughout his childhood. He also was reenacting the feeling that he had been thrown out of the family and abandoned. In fact, his mother had harbored strong wishes to get rid of him. At one point, when he was in an uncontrollable rage and began to destroy objects, I firmly stated, "Stop throwing things away or I'll throw *you* out." He stopped in his tracks, appeared frightened, scanned my face, slowly began to smile, and both of us broke into laughter. He gleefully began to chant, "I throw you out." After this session, his mother reported that Gerald had begun to verbalize and be more cooperative.

Recognizing that my own mounting rage toward Gerald was congruent with his own rage and that of the mother, I was able to express my rage, my inclination to throw him out, and to reflect his rage in a way that indicated to Gerald that I could be like him and his mother, but without disastrous consequences. The mutual laughter represented the fact that both he and I had mastered a difficult mutual problem.

A Passive–Aggressive Boy

A 9-year-old boy whose father had deserted him and his mother maintained considerable repressed rage that was channeled into passive–aggressive maneuvers. Weekly treatment sessions seemed to move very slowly. From time to time he seemed to like to have his mother come into the sessions because she tended to talk for him, he could reveal negative feelings toward her with little fear of retaliation, and it gave him a sense of a reintegrated family. In time Billy increasingly turned his anger toward me, especially in the presence of his mother who seemed completely shocked by his outbursts to me. Even though I explained to her the process of negative transference, she could not comprehend the intensity of his rage. The following is a typical excerpt from a session:

P: You ruin my day.
T: How?
P: By making me come here.
T: Why don't you stop coming here?
P: I can't.
T: Why not?
P: My mother and you make me come here—but I'm not coming here anymore.
T: How are you going to arrange that?
P: I'm going to kill you—smash your face. You are the most rotten person I know.
T: When do you plan to do this?
P: I don't know. You'll see. I'd like to do it right now. And you deserve it because you've ruined my life.
T: How did I do that?
P: By making me come here.

After considerably more vituperative attacks, I told Billy and his mother that it was time to leave.

Billy simply got up and said airily, "Goodby Dr. Marshall, see you next week." In the ensuing weeks, he continued to vent his aggression toward me—generally with the theme that I ruined his life. At one point I asked "Who has ruined you more, your mother or me?" He indicated, in the presence of his mother, that she was an angel compared with me and his only quarrel with her was that she wasn't able to control me. Later when I asked him, "Who's worse, me or your father," he was able for the first time to begin exploring his feelings toward his father.

The therapy was successful only because I was able to sustain Billy's attacks toward me which then allowed for a transference interpretation.

An Intellectualized Asthmatic

In the first interview, Evan, a sad-faced 9-year-old, sat on the edge of his chair anxiously rubbing his hands. In a British accent, precise pronunciation, and highly articulate manner he put forth his problem. "I have asthma. It interferes with everything and prevents me from doing what I want. I wheeze when I worry. I try to forget and think of nice things in the future. I don't want to talk about my worries—help me forget them."

After exploring with him his idea that forgetting worries would cure his asthma, I agreed, after his insistence, to help him. In subsequent sessions he enjoyed talking about his "excitement" which helped fend off asthmatic attacks. When he turned to talk about his worries, I reminded him of his not wanting to discuss them. Evan's "excitement" was related to his being with his parents usually in travel and vacations, while his "worry" seemed to be associated with being alone. Evan seemed to suffer from emotional neglect because both of his parents were highly intellectualized and professional, and devoted themselves to their work and studies. Evan substantiated the characterological embeddedness of this neglect in an incident involving a guinea pig in the playroom. The guinea pig began screeching and whistling for attention and food. I asked Evan what we should do. Blandly, Evan shrugged and replied, "He can wait until we're finished." It seemed clear that in his neglect of the guinea pig's needs Evan was identifying with his parents' unresponsiveness to his own needs. In another instance Evan talked about his annoyance with a screeching bird in a zoo. "It made too much noise. My parents don't like noise. They don't like pets because they make noise and we have to take care of them."

Evan proposed the idea that "bad thoughts" led to shameful feelings which in turn led to wheezing. I reminded him of our agreement about not talking about worrisome things. He brushed aside my joining statement and went on to discuss his father's asthma when a child, summarizing with, "He probably had bad thoughts."

After about 2 months of work Evan reported good control of his wheezing which he attributed to his work with breathing exercises and his ability to avoid bad thoughts and think good thoughts. At this point, in reaction to my silences, Evan reported no thoughts and then developed an obsessive worry. "What's going to happen next?" I had the impression that my silences were perceived as transferential abandonments and produced the precursor to his asthmatic attacks. Evan then talked about terminating. In a countertransferential statement I told him that *I* would feel sad and lonely if he didn't continue. Apparently, in reaction to my mishandling of his transference resistance Evan in his next session, firmly and coldly stated that he wheezed no more, and that he had convinced his parents that he should terminate.

In retrospect, the countertransference resistance was an induced identification with Evan's sadness and loneliness which should not have been communicated. One might consider that I was not fully in touch with the extent of Evan's melancholia. Moreover, a complicating countertransference feeling was wanting to care for him as his parents had not cared.

Fortunately, Evan apparently forgave my mistake and allowed me another chance to help him. Two months later he reappeared in my office stating that his wheezing had returned. I asked him how I might better help him this time. Evan retorted clearly, "This time let's go about it scientifically" (i.e., with no feelings involved). Taking Evan's cue we made a systematic study of the conditions under which wheezing occurred with my taking considerable notes. We set up hypotheses, tested them and established principles such as:

Forget about wheezing.

Think amusing thoughts.

Read.

Watch TV.

Have only one thing in mind.

Forget about certain thoughts and feelings.

Start the above when beginning to wheeze or as soon after as possible because the longer the wheezing goes on, the more effort and time it will take to stop.

Wheezing can be transformed into sneezing. Start sneezing by (a) catching cold, (b) think of sneezing instead of wheezing, (c) forget about wheezing and just sneeze.

Have fun by: playing chess with father, reading, going to school, being in my room at home, and having mother at home.

An important event resulted in Evan's expression of anger at me with a concomitant improvement in his asthmatic attacks. A day before his session, he called asking if he could cancel because he wanted to go to a birthday party. While not forbidding him to attend the party, I insisted that he come to the session. When he came to his session, his intellectual defenses gave way to his feelings of fury about my not caring for him, my neglecting his feelings, etc.

While we were in the process of discussing and analyzing the cessation of his wheezing after attacking me, Evan's parents were rather abruptly transferred by their company to another part of the country where he continued his treatment.

An Aggressive Asthmatic

Paul was a 9-year-old bright, frisky, youngster whose asthmatic attacks controlled the entire family. As treatment progressed and he could trust the therapist, Paul slowly began to act out his underlying hostility about the erratic care he received in his early life. At first subtly mischievous and teasing, Paul soon demonstrated the pleasure he experienced in expressing his aggression. The therapist, in calling attention to Paul's developing pleasure in aggressive words and acts, dubbed him "King of the Meanies." Delighting in the therapist's intervention, Paul agreed to work out "Paul's Rules of Meanness." Some of the "rules" he spontaneously verbalized. Others were determined by the therapist on the basis of Paul's behavior.

Try to drive others crazy by staying on the move.
Keep telling the other person that he stinks and you are better.
Keep criticizing others, especially when they feel they have done something well.
Mess up.
Threaten to break and ruin other's property.
Do not do what somebody asks you.
Constantly threaten to leave and desert the other person.
Bite the other person.
Shoot darts at him.
Make fun of how he talks.
Scream.

The last five came in fairly quick succession ending in Paul's screaming at the therapist for not letting him act out the meanness. Oral sadism as part of Paul's asthma is evident in the sequence. With the list, we were subsequently able to discuss Paul's fear of expressing his rage to his frustrating abandoning parents, and how he converted his feelings into wheezing. Moreover, his constant high level of activity was also interpreted as an identification with his parents who were "always on the move."

A Silly Giggler

Children, especially between the ages of 7 and 12, usually enjoy the therapist listing behavioral and characterological traits, especially if the therapist puts them in a favorable light. Listing involves hypervaluation and sometimes tutoring and mirroring. In the process of cataloging, the child usually veers onto significant material. For example, an 11-year-old revealed somewhat ashamedly that she was considered to be "silly and stupid" by her mother, teachers, and peers. During the sessions Sue indeed acted in an immature (silly and stupid) manner. I asked her the following, "What was wrong with being silly and stupid?" She did not know. "How did you become silly and stupid?" Sue could not answer that either. Then I asked, "Could you teach me how to become silly and stupid?" When she questioned me about why I wanted to learn how to be silly and stupid, I told her that all too often I was serious and tried too hard to be smart and that I had trouble getting out of that mode. Also, I told her, "I work with children who don't ever have fun and study all the time. I could help them if I could teach them to be silly and stupid." So she began to list avidly and gleefully. Each item was explained extensively and with many examples.

Do the opposite of what everybody else does.
Make stupid noises—like passing wind.
Make silly and stupid faces (which she demonstrated).
When somebody asks you a question say, "I don't know" or "I forget."
Hurt yourself by banging your head and kicking hard things to get sore toes and sore head. Hit your head.
Throw things around.
Rattle things and make noise.
Answer all questions with the same silly stupid word. Answer like a cat or dog.
Act like a chimpanzee.
Answer both "yes" and "no" to the same question.

At this point Sue became serious and discussed her mother's "silly" behavior and ended up by resolving to "give up being silly and stupid." I challenged this intention with "Why do you want to do that?" She replied," "Well, at least you must stop being silly and stupid when somebody tells you to."

In essence, Sue conducted a study of an important aspect of

her character. While making up the list we were able to trace her "silly and stupid" manner in her feelings about her "silly and stupid" sister who was borne by her "silly and stupid" mother.

Later in therapy Sue again became aware of her inappropriate behavior, particularly her forced gales of laughter, falling off her chair, and tension. She termed her behavior "silly," but insisted she was having a wonderful time. I enjoined her to tell me "how to be silly." The following list emerged, each point offered with gaiety.

Start laughing.
Snort.
Hiccough.
Scream that you have hiccoughs.
Fall on floor laughing—off chair preferred.
Sing a song on the floor.
Sing about worms.
Somebody screams "There's a worm under you."
Tickle somebody until they laugh and fall on the floor. Sit on them and holler, "Rape!" "When someone comes running kick 'em in the dickem easily. They get mad and pout."

Following this session, we were able to discuss how her excitement related to being bathed by her father, perhaps watching him in the bath, and the bathing of her brother.

A "Gang" Delinquent

A 15-year-old boy, referred because of school truancy, insolence in school, academic failure, and overall oppositionalism, had psychological testing suggesting that his construction and deteriorating behavior were functions of underlying depression. Pat saw no need for treatment. He did, however, agree to come for a few sessions only because of pressure from his mother and school. In general, he spoke with an exaggeratedly confident manner suggestive of his underlying lack of security. However, in describing his friends whom he termed "Greasers" he perked up and revealed a liveliness and involvement not previously apparent. He proudly contrasted his "Greasers" with the "Potheads" who were devoted to drugs, and with the "Fags" or "Neutrals" who studied, worked hard, and generally were characterized by adherence to the "Protestant Ethic," or had no identity to Pat. I demonstrated a real interest in his analysis of the social factions, their characteristics, and relationships. I became particularly interested in the characteristics and functions of the Greasers. Pat listed the "Code of the Greasers" for me.

> Wear leather jackets.
>
> Never go to class—hang out.
>
> Cops always after you.
>
> Don't do drugs.
>
> Smoke cigarettes.
>
> Be interested in mechanics, like bikes (motorcycles) and cars.

While not making any judgments about the characteristics of the different groups, I did praise Pat for his ability to paint such a clear picture of the adolescent scene. As Pat was inspired to talk about the groups, he was clear that his word pictures began to have some impact on him in that he began to puzzle about the value for him in being part of any of the groups. While maintaining a basic allegiance to the "Greasers," Pat had second thoughts about the advisability of being chased by the cops and have school authorities "hassling" him.

In this therapeutic situation, I could not affirm many of the items in the Greasers' code except "Don't do drugs." However, I was able to create a positive atmosphere relative to his ability to describe interesting social phenonema rather clearly. As Pat talked, he clarified his values for himself and made differentiations and decisions that helped him define himself relative to others. One is reminded of the story cited by Watzlawick et al. (1967) "The fable of the cockroach who asked the centipede how he managed to move his hundred legs with such elegant ease and perfect co-ordination. From that moment on, the centipede could not walk anymore" (p. 237).

A Delusional Child

In the initial session, Walter was quiet, cautious, had no concept of why he was present, and gave unimaginative, concrete answers. The 10-year-old boy, while calmly playing with his fingers, indicated that he had difficulty in controlling his limbs which led to his getting in trouble with his parents. I asked him to make up a story about what his fingers were doing. He proceeded in a hesitant manner about a car that fell off a cliff, exploded, and burned. Another car teetering on the edge finally fell and was badly damaged. He then accelerated the action and described two planes crashing, the presence of battleships and submarines, and finally stated, "A big battle is brewing"—meanwhile gesticulating with his finger.

For the next two sessions Walter backed away from the fantasy life. I asked him how I could help him control his feet, hands, and fingers. He decided that tossing a football would provide him with beneficial practice.

It appeared that Walter had revealed too much of his inner turmoil in the initial session and wanted to reassure himself of his control in the therapy session. The therapeutic conflict involved reflecting or confronting Walter with the anxiety-arousing turmoil within himself or silently noting his state and allowing the natural defenses to evolve. Having decided on the latter course, the therapeutic conflict was to interpret the defense-resistance or join it. Knowing the fragile state of Walter's ego it was deemed best to support it by supporting and joining his defenses. The possible complication of such a maneuver is that the patient senses that the therapist cannot cope with the chaotic feelings hence may be made more anxious, have no faith in the therapist, or may withdraw from therapy. My experience has been that with outpatients who are seen once or twice a week and where the patient's ego is in a weakened or borderline state, it is far safer to side with the ego defenses and limit, in a measured and controlled way, the experience of feared affect and impulses. In an institutional setting, where the child can be seen more frequently and where behavior can be controlled, a more interpretive approach might be taken according to Masterson or Rinsley.

The joining maneuver appeared to work successfully, for in the next session Walter began the revelation of his delusional fantasy life. In the therapeutic interchange, the therapist took the stance that his fantasies were real and asked questions about elements in the fantasy and *not* about Walter's ego state. This approach is congruent with Spotnitz's (1969) distinction between ego-oriented and object-oriented questions and similar to Ritvo's (1978) suggestion that the therapist's interventions remain within the context and metaphor of the play. Lindner's (1955) case of the Jet Propelled Couch is also analogous to the acceptance of the patient's experience, reports, and records.

Walter stated that there had been a "Bad Guy" and a "Good Guy" in his head. They had been present since he breathed in germs when his mother was pregnant with him. The Bad Guy made sneak attacks, cut telephone lines, destroyed equipment, and flooded basements where important equipment was stored. Walter was in search of sentries who would not betray him. Walter also revealed that he would obtain tanks, planes, and other equipment by breathing in.

The transferential statement about needing trustful sentries was well noted and used for a very long time in the treatment. Children, fairly early in treatment, reveal to therapists how they can best help and the most appropriate transference role to assume. Walter preferred that the therapist act as an observer, sometimes as a consultant, and never as a controlling agent.

The therapist was constantly alert to the historic significance of the delusional material. In essence, Walter was revealing his impressions of his preverbal experience. The parents were able to verify that the father was very instrumental in rearing Walter. When Walter was three months old, Walter's maternal grandmother, who had terminal cancer, was taken into the home and cared for by the mother until the grandmother's death when Walter was 13 months old. During this period Walter's mother, according to the father, underwent a personality change that turned her from a patient, loving person to a relatively bitter and cynical one.

Walter continued in his explicit description of the conflict between the Good Guy and the Bad Guy while the therapist questioned for clarification:

> "Not a war now. He controls all my lines of communication through my brain. He doesn't like me—he hates me (T: Since when?). Started hating me years ago—I don't remember. At night he goes to sleep. He rarely fights at night. He might take a vacation. But he might use computers at night. He blocks my brain lanes with his computer. Bad Guy gets his supplies through my mouth and nose—smuggled in with the Good Guy's. Maybe the Bad Guy's supplies come in my rear end when I'm changing clothes. The Bad Guy controls my mouth, lips, and voice box—makes me say things I don't want to. My vision and hearing is not controlled unless I'm doing a lot of stuff. The Good Guy's and Bad Guy's cables meet and join together in the central power supply. The Good Guy's cables are all worn out. Something went wrong when they were first tried out. They were used too much. They can be fixed (Therapist: "How?"). Since the central power is in the middle, you could cut the Bad Guy's power and direct it to the Good Guy (Therapist: "How could this be done?"). Sneak information in quietly and supplies in slowly. The Bad Guy should be put in electric and cement walls under a prison. Then the Good Guy could get some power."

As Walter clearly reconstructed his infantile experience, he just as clearly communicated how the therapist could help him. The general context and use of symbols drifted slowly in the direction of reality. For example, just before Thanksgiving Walter indicated that both the Good Guy and Bad Guy liked food and that there would be a truce on Thanksgiving while both went to his belly for a feast.

Walter revealed that the Bad Guy had cut off most of the supplies coming through his mouth to the Good Guy. It certainly looked like the end of the Good Guy. None of my inquiries suggested any way the Good Guy could be saved—he would simply waste away, starve, and be taken over by the Bad Guy. I suggested to Walter that he start his own army as a means of possibly helping the Good Guy. Walter indicated that he had had no experience in starting an army. I asked him if I could be a "military adviser" especially since I had had some military experience.

Walter was very hesitant and cautious, indicating that this was a "top secret" operation. Walter decided that he would recruit deserters and adventurers "those who don't care who they fight for," but "they must be interrogated fully." He managed to find 3–4 rifles, and knives, made bows and arrows, put in supply orders to the Good Guy, and situated the little camp outside his brain, "near the passage of the lung."

Walter provided "on-the-spot coverage" to me implying that the core delusional material was becoming exhausted and that he now was spontaneously providing material more akin to fantasy, daydreams, and free association.

Walter's small force discovered a tank and 17 wounded men. He speculated about combing the battlefields for more wounded men, caring for them, and working them into his army. His men discovered an old abandoned headquarters building with computers, switches, arms, etc. He assumed that there had been many other armies in the past and that this HQ had belonged to the "Zodiac Army." He further speculated that the Good Guy and Bad Guy armies had been united at one time. He was able to affirm this through the use of a captured "Time Machine Viewer."

Over the course of the next 8 weeks Walter reported an increasing buildup of his army, a good independent source of supplies, and increasing number of victories. However, as he would become confident and discuss negotiations and victory, he would report increased vicious attacks by the "Bad Guy."

In the final battles, Walter would describe in graphic drawings the fierce battles, with special emphasis on sneak attacks, tricks, secret weapons he used. The latter was likely to be a reflection of his identification with the highly manipulative father and the therapist's position. Finally, Walter reported that his army and the Good Guys had won the war.

But there was more work to be done that coincided with two events: something of a positive nature about our work got to the parents from their counselor and then to Walter, and an acute family crisis.

The very next session, Walter reported that the Zodiacs had invaded at 8:30 P.M. on Saturday with a paralysis dream gun with bullets like atom bombs! The gun also forages supplies, guns, and bombs.

> "The Zodiacs joined with the Bad Guys to steal our secrets, take our supplies, and mouth and headache circuits. They have spies, found out secrets, taken all ammunition, fort, and half of the Good Guy forces was either captured, wounded or killed. The only possible way of surviving was to go back in the time machine to look for trapped forces."

After I "tightened security" with the parents' counselor and after the family crisis was resolved, Walter returned to a previous era through the time machine, gathered fresh forces, and won the war.

The first phase of treatment lasted about 1 year. During this time psychotic symptoms, observed in school and at home, disappeared. Gradually, he became more argumentative and obstinate, but with increasing good humor. School work improved slowly.

The next stage of therapy, which lasted 18 months, brought forth violent competition with the therapist in various board games where Walter sought to "slaughter," "smash," "dismember," etc. the therapist. Walter seldom spontaneously referred to the Good Guy–Bad Guy war. But when the therapist contrasted the therapeutic competition with previous events, Walter accepted the parallels amusedly.

The third stage of treatment, which lasted another 2 years, involved more direct discussion about his parents and brother (the Bad Guys) and his attempts to extricate himself from their control. He finally decided that he could function better outside of the home situation and opted for a boarding school where he conducted himself extremely well.

Before terminating therapy, Walter brought in a book report which, in rich literary and well-sublimated form, described a man who had learned to control and use the destructive forces within him while coming to terms with the fear and violence in the outside world.

There are several common denominators in these cases:

- The children manifested behavior that usually induced "negative" feelings and behavior in therapists. Common feelings are frustration, neglect, anger, guilt, and anxiety.
- The induced feelings usually represent the unconscious feelings of the patient to the therapist and earlier objects, or the early, harmful feelings of the parents to the patient.
- Therapeutic strategy was based on an understanding of the induced countertransference feelings.
- In no case was the provocative behavior (usually a significant defense-resistance) interpreted, analyzed, or otherwise challenged or attacked until late in treatment.
- The provocative behavior was met by the therapist with joining techniques that affirmed the patient's defenses and resistances.
- The therapeutic interventions produced a reduction of anxiety and yielding of defensive behavior, reduction of symptoms, and progress in treatment in terms of talking more about personal, affective material.

Chapter 6

ON THE CONCEPTS OF RESISTANCE AND COUNTERTRANSFERENCE IN PARENTAL GUIDANCE AND FAMILY THERAPY

Relying primarily on the classic psychoanalytic model of treatment of adults, child guidance workers in the 1930s and early 1940s generally focused on children and their intrapsychic and interpersonal problems. Problems of diagnosis and interest in determining dynamics seemed to dominate while methods of treatment were being evolved. As the therapists became more knowledgeable and perhaps overcame their own resistance to working with the mother, social workers were usually assigned to the guidance and treatment of the mother, while the child was usually assigned to a psychiatrist. The field was strongly influenced by D. Levy's (1939) study of the overprotective mother and Kestenberg's (1941) characterization of three types of mothers: the openly aggressive, the anxious, and the genuinely anxious. The late 1940s and early 1950s saw a burgeoning interest in mother–child relations with special emphasis on the "schizophrenogenic mother" juxtaposed with a passive, indifferent father.

Mothers were incorporated into treatment not only because general knowledge of mother–child relations was growing, but because child therapists became aware of the phenomenon of the mother who directly or indirectly sabotaged the child's treatment. One gets the impression that workers, without neglecting the gains made in treating children, turned to the mother as the major source of resistance, just as Freud focused on the phenomenon of resistance as undermining the efforts of the therapists. Gardner's *The Case Studies in Childhood Emotional Disabilities,* Vol. I (1953) and Vol. II (1956), typify the varidisciplinary approach to diagnosis and treatment of children on an outpatient and institutional basis.

The "simultaneous analysis" of mother and child drew considerable attention. K. Levy's (1960) report of the analysis of a mother coupled with Sprince's (1962) account of the corresponding analysis of the daughter provide the model of this era. A. Freud (1960), reporting on nine such analyses, challenged the simple notion that "most mental disturbances can be traced back to the disturbances of their parents." (p. 480). Another related finding was that not all the children showed direct reactions to the mother's pathology—that the children are affected *indirectly* as a function of the mother's limitations *qua* mothers. However, certain cases were "slowed up" or were "made impossible" (p. 481) when the child's pathology interlocked with the mother's pathology. Weiss et al. (1968) evolved the following principle: "To treat a child prior to object constancy is to treat the parent and child as a unit" (p. 648). In neurotic involvements, Weiss et al. recommend that the analyst set up lines of communication, define the limits of the contacts and "expand the parent's awareness so that transference and acting out are minimized."

Despite the fact that the first psychological treatment of a child was conducted with the full involvement of a father (the case of Little Hans), little in the literature indicated that fathers were being integrated into treatment plans. Several sources cited by Strean (1970) recommended the father's involvement, but there seemed to be little progress in this area until the tide of family therapy swept the father into the treatment situation. There are numerous reasons for the lack of the father's involvement such as working hours not coinciding with available treatment time, cultural mores that supported a division of labor, and roles that separated the father from the child care position etc. However, one may consider the hypothesis that the resistances keeping the father "outside" were supplemented and potentiated by the counterresistances of therapists.

Several specific situations are offered in terms of therapist dynamics: The preoedipal therapist, (a) who identifies with the child, invites the child's mother into treatment to care for the therapist, and ignores the existence of the father; or (b) who wants neither mother nor father in the picture so that the therapist may act out his or her countertransferences with the child. Those countertransferences may relate to therapists wanting freedom to play with children and to "save" them from the parental ogres, etc.

(2) The oedipal therapist, (a) who in the guise of treating the child maintains an unconscious erotic relationship with the mother and competes with the father by being an ideal father and husband. Frequently, this arrangement is diagnosed by the steady disillusionment of the mother about her mate and a deterioration in the marriage; or (b) who may invite the father in, but "dumps" on him or is competitive in such a way as to drive him out.

These counterresistances are usually apparent in the sameness of therapists' approach to new cases and the rigidity with which they cling to a particular arrangement even when treatment is obviously floundering.

The therapists who conceptualized only in dyadic terms (parent–therapist, child–parent), and especially those dealing with preoedipal children and parents, probably were having equivocal results or failure and were trying new treatment devices. Kramer and Byerly (1978) list four sources of resistance in the parents which must be resolved for progress to occur in the child's treatment: (a) narcissistic injury as a function of their not being able to help their child; (b) emotional reactions to the child's increasing independence; (c) inability to handle increased assertiveness and acting out of analytic material; (d) feeling left out because it is the parent who wants treatment. When therapists finally determined that the child's symptoms and ability to get well were a function of the integrity of the parental egos and of the marital relationship, qualitative changes were made in treatment concepts and procedures.

These insights emerged from the development of family

therapy. Operating out of field and systems theories, family therapists have been intrigued by the steadiness of equilibrium of certain families particularly when flagrant pathology exists. For example, in 1963 Haley observed, "When one person indicates a change in relation to another, the other will act upon the first so as to diminish and modify that change" (p. 189).

Jackson and Weakland (1971) posed the problem: "Why does pathological behavior or organization persist even under pressure to change? We have not solved this problem . . ." (p. 29). They go on to advance two explanatory ideas: (a) that circular and interactive double binds exist; (b) statements do not clarify but are "effectively but indirectly negotiated or 'disqualified'." (p. 29) The concept of disqualification is important because it psychologically annihilates the other person. Joining and mirroring are polar to disqualification because they seek to recognize and validate what the person feels at the edge of consciousness.

In attempting to circumnavigate the problem of resistance in families, Weakland (1976) seeks to exorcise the psychoanalytic conceptual devils,

> Put bluntly, a sizable part of our work on communication appears related to digging ourselves out of individual-centered, depth-psychological views of behavior, problems and therapy in which we originally were embedded, rather than to any elaborate creation of new view (p. 121).

He argues that the metapsychology of psychoanalysis is in itself a metaresistance to understanding family problems.

Many sociologists, such as K. Erikson (1964), and social psychologists who study the phenomena of dissonance, social judgment, attribution, and attitude–opinion change, appear to be working on the factors that produce consistency and change in behavior. Wylie's two volumes (1961, 1979) are monuments to the thousands of studies on the variables influencing self-concept, self-esteem, and their correlates. With some exceptions, there is limited but increasing use of concepts and information across these fields into psychotherapy and particularly psychoanalysis. Perhaps, in the future, bridges will be constructed across disciplines in order to better understand the phenomenon of equilibrium within the person and among persons. Levant (1980) has initiated rapprochement between social and clinician theorists. He discerns three paradigms: (a) the structural, which "describes the enduring organizational structure of the family and analyzes the underlying function and hierarchical relationship of the components" (p. 19). Parsons and Minuchin represent this model; (b) the process paradigm depicts the dynamic flow of interaction and emphasizes the interrelatedness of the players. The Chicago School of Sociology (G. H. Mead) and clinicians such as Bowen, Fogerty, Ackerman, and Satir are examples of the second model; (c) the historic paradigm views the development of the family over one or more generations. Role and developmental stage-task social theorists complement clinicians such as Framo and Bowen and psychoanalytically oriented clinicians.

Framo (1965) defined resistance as "the opposition against attempts to expose unconscious motives." (p. 177) He wisely notes that family therapists are prone to experience considerable disappointment at a "massive resistance stage" (p. 179) that occurs when the immediate crisis of the designated patient is past and evident strain in the family system is diminished. He cites five types of resistant families: (a) the passively uncooperative family that "wipes out" the therapist and evokes feelings of uselessness; (b) the family that produces repetitive material; (c) the family that clings to fixed roles and relationships; (d) the family that is afraid of abandoning infantile satisfactions; and (e) the family that cannot tolerate guilt. Framo categorizes types of resistance: (a) focus on designated patient's craziness; (b) avoidance of talk about the marital relationship; (c) absurd exaggeration of therapist's comments; (d) deflection from intrapsychic explorations; (e) strong sense of loyalty to family; and (f) "protection" of family members. Other resistances based more on countertransferences are: (a) importance of family in the community; (b) "well" siblings who have distanced themselves from the family; (c) "sweet, grey-haired mothers"; (d) the fragility of families based on considerable trauma; and (e) wide cultural differences between family and therapist.

Sonne et al. (1962), who prefer to work with the whole family, view the "absent-member maneuver" as a major source and symptom of resistance to family therapy. Bell (1975) handles this resistance by walking out—presumably mirroring the resistance. Satir (1964) warns against approaching the marital problem when parents can only focus on the "problem child." Chassin et al. (1974), given parents who have a disturbed relationship but wish only to talk of the child, recommend a child-focused management program that enlists the parents' cooperation and involvement. This approach avoided resistance while deepening the working relationship.

Haley (1971) in advocating a "positive view" advises the following:

> For example, a beginning family therapist working with the family of a schizophrenic observed the mother pat her son on the behind. He could not overlook this opportunity to help her by interpreting this behavior as the product of an incestuous desire, with the result that mother and son avoided each other even more than previously. A more experienced family therapist could probably have congratulated the mother on being able to show some affection toward her son. (p. 233)

Tongue in cheek, Haley (1963) proclaims:

> A resistance interpretation falls in the general class of "turning it back on the patient" ploys. All attempts, particularly successful ones, to place the analyst one-down can be interpreted as resistance to treatment. The patient is made to feel that it is *his* fault that therapy is going badly. Carefully preparing in advance, the skillful analyst informs the patient in the first interview that the path to happiness is difficult and he will at times resist getting well and indeed may even resent the analyst for helping him. (p. 196)

Palazzoli et al. (1978), using communications theory, attempt to forestall and then bypass the resistances in families by the use of "positive connotation." This device consists of positive statements about the families' homeostasis and about the individual's contribution to the family's cohesiveness and stability. After gaining the trust of and access to the family, the therapists devise paradoxical prescriptions based on the dynamics of the family.

Whitaker et al. (1965) address themselves to the countertransference of the family therapist who they feel is more prone to countertransference reactions than any other kind of therapist, particularly when confronted with schizophrenics and their families. They define countertransference as the "distorted feelings of the therapist" that resonate not only from the transference of the family, but from subgroups within the family. Moreover, Whitaker allows himself to identify with the patient and experientially reverses roles so that he can feel into the patient's phenomenology and experience the patient in the role of the therapist. Countertransference is viewed as necessary but nontherapeutic. That is, to treat the family successfully, the therapist must *evolve* and then *resolve* the very deep feelings that the family evokes. As in an earlier paper, Whitaker et al. (1962) indicate that consistent resistances to cure are schizophrenics' preoccupation with sacrificing themselves to preserve some important aspect of family life such as the marriage of the parents. This conceptualization is similar to Spotnitz's (1969) major contention that schizophrenics, in assuming a narcissistic defense, sacrifice their own ego to preserve the object. Searles (1975) has also developed a similar idea in discussions of the child caring for the parent and the patient treating the therapist.

Several techniques are provided for resolving countertransference: (a) use more than one therapist; (b) maintain an overview of the family as a whole while moving in and out of relationships with individuals and subgroups; (c) leave the initiative for the conduct of the interview to the family; (d) use a consultant in the interviews.

Stierlin (1975) focuses on the family myth in his understanding of resistance families. Analogizing the myth of the family to the defense of the individual, he sees the myth providing a coherent, rational organization for the family's cognitive, interpersonal, and affective needs. Not only does the myth satisfy the family's needs to hide and distort reality, but it attempts to mislead the therapist. Technically, Stierlin advises that therapists build up the family members' trust in them. As the therapist gains trust through "involved impartiality," the family members release their transferences from each other and make the therapist the target in a classic mode. Caution is advised in siding with the "sick" victimized adolescent, the "rebellious" adolescent, or the victimized parent.

Carter and Orfanidis (1976) advocate a training device wherein student family therapists attempt to resolve their families' problems, in an effort not only to acquaint students emotionally with family dynamics but to help them resolve and subsequently prevent countertransferences.

The position of this book is that the family is a system governed by the principle of homeostasis. The familial homeostasis is helped in maintaining its equilibrium by the individual homeostatic needs of each member. That is, the protective, survival, and homeostatic aspects of each member's defense-resistances (discussed in Chapter 2) provide constant feedback to each other's systems and the meta (familial) system. The resistances of the family are viewed not judgmentally but with respect for their function and strength. The resistances are to be understood, and resolved so as to maintain the health of the system and its component members. Moreover, the countertransference feelings remain central in the process. The following chapter outlines a method termed Sequence Therapy which attempts to approach the resistances of the family and its members in a constructive manner.

Chapter 7

THE RESOLUTION OF RESISTANCES IN THE FAMILY

The Clinical Sequence and Sequence Therapy*

The Initial Contact—The Telephone Call

The fact that many people telephone for an appointment they then fail to keep suggests that this early contact is of prime importance and is worth study from the standpoint of resistance.

Since therapists have the minimum of information on which to rely, they must make quick decisions in order to make it easier for the parents (and child) to keep the appointment. After the parent (usually the mother) introduces herself and provides some information about the child and the referral source, the therapist can ask the question, "When would you like to come in?" The vague pronoun "you" allows the mother to provide her own interpretation and choice as to whom she thinks should be involved. If the mother makes an assumption or says nothing about who should come in, no challenge is made and the therapist must be ready to see any combination of the family at the first interview. Usually the mother will ask who should come in. Without any other information, and if the child is young, the therapist

*The term "Sequence Therapy" was suggested by Simone Marshall.

may ask the mother for her opinion or ask both parents to come in without the child. If an adolescent is involved, a good rule of thumb is to ask the mother, father, and teenager to come in.

In discussing the time for the appointment, considerable important information may come to light. In fact, sometimes major family dynamics can be revealed. For example, a mother may say, "I never know when my husband will be home" or "He's away on a trip and I'm not sure when he'll be available" or "He always works late. Can you give us a late evening appointment?" In the initial phone call, the therapist may discern that there is a symbiotic relationship between mother and child. In this instance, especially when the father seems unavailable, ask the mother and child to come in. Several cases have been lost at this point because the fusion between mother and child was not respected. The mother may get the impression that if the child is excluded from the initial interview, the therapist seeks to break the symbiosis prematurely. The therapist must keep in mind that, unconsciously, the mother is not only calling for help for her child *per se,* but wants help with other problems such as her marriage or her own problems.

In general, and especially if the child or adolescent appears with the parents for the interview, an hour and a half may be allotted. If, during this time, the therapist feels that a shorter interview is more appropriate he or she can exercise that option. On the other hand, many therapists insist that the parents should conform to a regular schedule from the beginning.

Returning to the question of the appointed time, the most cooperative and least resistant response the therapist can receive is, "When is your earliest open time?" or "We can come in anytime." After the therapist indicates a time, the cooperative and motivated mother will indicate that she will make it her business to be there. Usually, and especially with resistant parents, several appointment times may have to be offered. Sometimes the mother suggests a time. The therapist carefully observes this transaction, especially the reasons given for not being able to attend. For example, one mother refused a time because of a hairdresser's appointment. Another refused several appointments because of her complex duties for her family. Other mothers tend to make appointment time revolve around the convenience of the father, school, religious activities, sports, etc. If no appointment time can be agreed upon, the therapist may join the resistance and also test the motivation for treatment by asking the mother to call back at a specified time within a week.

Questions by the mother about fees, type of treatment, length of treatment, etc., can be met by a question such as, "Would you mind discussing this question at our first meeting?" A question about the source of the referral may be appropriate. Questions by the therapist should be restricted to establishing an appointment time and quietly studying any resistance patterns that emerge. Questions pertaining to the presenting problem are generally uncalled for because this may unleash an amount of anxiety in the parent that cannot be resolved over the phone, thereby producing deleterious effects. On the other hand, sometimes one senses that a general question about the nature of the problem is necessary to establish the emotional contact necessary to enable the prospective patient to keep the appointment.

Gurman (1980) has provided a brief discussion of the problems and procedures of a family therapist in the initial phone contact. He offers practical and detailed accounts of handling resistances to convening the family.

Ekstein and Friedman (1971) share their experience in the initial procedures of what they term "psychotherapeutic diagnosis" (p. 296). As if they had resistance in mind, they immediately search for "an assessment of how these very forces that led to the illness can be utilized as agents for the cure." (p. 296) Not primarily looking for a diagnostic label, the purpose of the assessment is to find a way that the family can enter an appropriate treatment program.

Palazzoli et al. (1978), in a good description of handling the initial contact with the family, consider that professionals should handle the entire process because of the rich clinical data provided by the inquiry.

The Initial Interview

The initial interview, especially with the parents or family, is crucial in determining whether a family will continue treatment.

On one hand there are families who, truly interested and cooperative in the therapeutic endeavor, are reassured when they sense that a therapist is willing and able to help them. On the other hand, some families who sense that the therapist is interested in changing the equilibrium will quickly abandon contact with him or her. Therefore, the therapist must make a prompt appraisal of the readiness for change. With the former family the therapist may, in all good faith, communicate a degree of optimism about feasibility for change. With the latter, the therapist may communicate a need for more information, bewilderment, or even a sense of helplessness in order to foster continued contacts. Furthermore, the resistant family will frequently ask, "What shall we do until the next session?" or "What changes should be made?" To reassure the family that the therapist is not going to be placed in the position of controller or change-maker, he or she should recommend that no change be made or ask what kind of changes the family would like to make. With this approach, the therapist is not pulled into making premature judgments about the rightness or wrongness of the family's activities.

Haley (1973) avoids resistance by choosing the system unit of the family that will best respond to interventions. He bypasses the question of resistance by using the strategic entrance that will yield the most limited resistance and maximal cooperation. For example, he has the option of approaching through the child, the father and child, the mother and child, the mother and father, and the whole family. He has the additional option of focusing on tasks for the strategic unit chosen.

Types of Parents

Following are descriptions of some types of parents and the respective entrances selected to establish a working relationship.

The Anxious–Devoted Parents

The initial consultation was with the parents who gave a detailed history of their 9-year-old son. The mother seemed particularly distressed during the first part of the interview. Although she described considerable pathology, she was not sure whether her son was ill and needed treatment. Her experience with physicians and pediatricians had led her to believe that she worried too much about him and that he would "grow out of it." When I acknowledged with her that indeed Saul had been suffering since infancy and that he needed treatment, she broke out crying, "Thank God somebody sees how sick he's been." This immediate joining (validation) of the mother's long-term feeling established a positive relationship that helped to tide over later difficult situations. The clinician, in the first interview, should make some effort to ascertain the parents' initial type and level of resistance and relate to it appropriately. Where the parents are highly anxious over their child, their concern can be acknowledged and treatment can usually begin immediately because their resistance to treatment is not manifested.

The Denying-Treatment Resistant Parents

Another type of parent, polar to the case described above, believes that nothing is seriously wrong with their child. They usually are present at the behest of court or school—after many years of difficulty. This type of parent with ample illustrative case material has been described by Strean (1970), Feldman (1958), and Love and Mayer (1959).

Frequently, the child's behavior is ego-syntonic with the parents' conscious and/or unconscious value system. The parent's own disturbed childhood represents a "superego lacunae" acted out by the child. Frequently, the child is the scapegoat for the family's problems. The interviewer attempts to discern the reasons for the parents' resistance to recognizing pathology. As they reel off the behavior that others find pathological, he joins them with such questions as "What's wrong with that?" or "What makes the principal think that's wrong?" The parents tend to respond with answers that make it apparent to them that something is wrong. Frequently, in more defensive parents, particularly the father, the answer is put in terms of his own childhood or adolescent difficulties. A light comment by the interviewer such as "like father, like son" or "a chip off the old block" with a follow-up such as "Well, you seem to have survived without psychotherapy" usually produces a disclaimer wherein the father tells more about his life. In many instances, a learning disability seems to have been transmitted from parent to child and the parent will indicate how he had suffered, perhaps mastered the problem, or still is plagued by its residues.

The Doubting Parents

Another type of parents are in doubt about the necessity for treatment. Frequently sophisticated, with some knowledge of psychotherapy (pro and con), and sometimes scientifically oriented, they search for objective signs that their child needs treatment. The interviewer may also express doubts and suggest psychological studies. The presentation of the data may be conducted in a didactic manner with full explanation of the tests until the parents are satisfied. One couple asked me in detail how I would treat their child. I began to explore their concern but found that they were becoming annoyed at my probes. I noted my own annoyance at their challenge to my ability to treat their child and resented the implied control. Rather than get onto countertransferential ground in the first session, I evaded the competence–control issue and responded to their request for information. In effect, I mirrored their intellectual resistance in that I gave a technical lecture on my probable approach to the child until they began to yawn and talk to each other. It turned out later that they resented the need for treatment and the loss of control over the child.

Parents Who Disagree About Treatment

So far, the parents have been discussed as they operate as a compatible dyad. Parents who disagree about diagnosis, severity of illness, and need for treatment, present special problems. This is frequently the case where the mother comes in alone for the initial interview, either making an excuse for the father or openly stating that he is not in favor of treatment. The father should come in as soon as possible in an attempt to discern the causes of his resistance. If this does not occur, the child, particularly a boy, will at some time begin to act out the father's resistance. Sometimes the mother's word about her husband's negative attitudes cannot be taken at face value. In one instance, the wife described the father as an "uncaring brute." This was true, but only in his relationship to her. Later, when the father finally came in, he was hurt and angry at having been left out of the treatment situation and proved to be very interested in and helpful to his son.

The One-Parent Family

Increasingly often, the mother may come in with her child or by herself. Although manifestly talking about her child, usually, in distress over a loss of her husband, she is covertly sizing up the therapist in terms of his or her ability to help her handle her own life in general. Any attempt to uncover this defense is usually most unkind and destructive. When this defense is joined, the mother, whose defenses are slight, will fairly soon tell the therapist of her more personal concerns and ask for individual therapy for herself. Where the reactive hurt or pathology is deeper, the mother will cling for a longer time to her cover story and discuss her child or children. In these instances, the mother will almost invariably bring herself into the sessions with the child or teenager. While many therapists view this as being controlling and manipulating on her part, I see this as a cooperative move because she is placing herself closer to the position of primary patient. When the mother dumps the child on the therapist and only reluctantly comes in for "parent guidance," the resistances are more profound and the prognosis more dim.

Sequence Therapy

Sequencing with one-parent families probably represents its simplest form. The basic idea of sequence therapy is to *work* with those defense-resistances of the family system that most threaten therapeutic progress. The word "work" is chosen, consistent with Freud's (1940[1938a]) statement that, "the *overcoming*[1] of resistances is the part of our work that requires the most time and greatest trouble" (p. 179). Considerable care must be taken to *diagnose* the source and type of resistance that needs to be worked on. The clinician should be prepared to see any combination of family members including the whole family. If the clinician does not have the skills, for example, to resolve a marital problem blocking treatment of the child, the couple may be referred for consultation with a colleague. Considerable care must be taken to *select* the technique that will best resolve the resistance.

Case Illustrations

A One-Parent Family

Mrs. E., whose husband had been killed 4 years prior to consultation, voiced considerable concern about her 15-year-old son, Ed, whose behavior had been deteriorating over a 2–3-year period. Ed's attendance and grades at school were declining and he was becoming more violent at home and school. Clinical and psychological examination revealed a young man whose narcissism, underlying depression, and identification with his father were leading him toward self-destruction. Several sessions with Ed promptly established a narcissistic transference. When positive feelings from an object transference threatened, Ed sought

[1]Freud used the word "resolve" in his *Studies in Hysteria,* but dropped its usage and tended to use more forceful verbs. In this book, the word "resolve" is preferred because it is a more neutral word and has more meanings than "overcome" and does not necessarily imply violence. According to Webster's Third New International Dictionary, "overcome" means "to get the better of: surmount, conquer, subdue" and "to affect or influence so strongly as to make physically helpless or emotionally distraught: overpower, overwhelm." Synonym is "conquer." "Resolve" on the other hand has the following meanings: (a) to separate or break up, change or convert by disintegration, reduce (b) to cause to disintegrate, break into bits or separate into constituent elements (c) to dissipate. Synonyms are given as "analyze" and "solve."

to leave therapy. At the same time, he insisted that his mother needed treatment more than he because she screamed uncontrollably and lapsed into apathy. Moreover, Ed's self-destructive behavior began to abate. At this point, several joint sessions occurred with a focus on the mother–son relationship. Issues of mutual control dominated. Ed's attendance became erratic and then ceased. Mrs. E., however, attended every weekly session, but used the time to understand her son and to effect a therapeutic atmosphere at home. She worked consistently on her own lack of control and her defenses against depression in a projective manner, i.e., through discussions of Ed's delayed mourning reaction and his displaced anger. Although Ed never again appeared for sessions, his progress paralleled his mother's. As the dependent–hostile relationship was resolved, Ed found himself an excellent job with an understanding boss and Mrs. E. found a boyfriend. The basic personality structures were not changed, but the interpersonal situation was shifted so that individuation could take place.

Sequencing was relatively simple in this situation. Ed's resistance to living took priority and was resolved by the evolution of a narcissistic transference to the therapist. As his resistance to an object transference mounted, attention was turned to the resistance that mother and son had in communicating with each other in a cooperative manner. As they worked through their identity and control problems, the emphasis shifted to Mrs. E.'s resistance to giving up her long-term mourning for her husband which was being acted out in her symbiotic relationship to her son.

The factor that seems to complicate and lengthen the treatment in similar one-parent families is the degree of pathology that had existed in the marriage. When one spouse divorces, deserts, or dies, there is a tendency to reenact the pathological marital relationship with one of the children. The eldest child of the sex of the lost parent tends to take up where he or she left off. In several cases where a sadistic father deserted a masochistic mother, the son eventually mirrored the father's behavior. Considerably more priority had to be given to the mother's resistance to giving up her masochistic position. The evoked countertransference sequence is usually that the male therapist first feels idolized and idealized by the child but particularly by the mother, and the therapist then slowly comes to resent the mother in particular ways and is tempted to abandon or cudgel her in a manner attributed to the husband. The dynamics of boys who have lost their fathers amount to a belated mourning reaction. In order to fend off depression, they act out their identification with the father and recreate him within themselves.

Resistance of an Adolescent Girl Potentiated by Parental Resistance

Sue, a bright 14-year-old girl subject to migraines and hysterical anesthesias, believed that her illnesses were related to her father's coldness and preference for a younger sister. She was not sure of the connection but was certain that if he became warmer toward her, she would get better. Rather than analyze her internal resistances, and wait for the oedipal transference to evolve, I decided to join her defense-resistance and subsequently spent 3–4 months helping her explore and analyze her father's life. The rationale for this approach was related to (a) the degree of anxiety and embarrassed blocking when talking about herself; (b) a sincere interest she had in understanding and helping her father; and (c) a sense that something was amiss not only in the father–daughter relationship but in the father's character. Ultimately, Sue convinced her father to enter treatment, at which point she breathed with relief, "Now we can talk about me." Sue did have a valid sense about the father, for we discovered that the father, who early in his life had devotedly cared for a schizophrenic sister, had transferred that care to Sue when she was born, and then dropped Sue presumably to prevent a schizophrenia in Sue's younger sister.

A Borderline Family

Family therapy is not feasible in certain types of families. These families are characterized by two or more of the following: (a) intensive scapegoating; (b) considerable borderline pathology; (c) mutual destructiveness when together; (d) emotional estrangement among members of the family. These families usually insist that one person, frequently a child or adolescent, is sick and must be treated outside of the context of the family. Not withstanding the recommendations of therapists such as Whitaker in handling treatment-resistant families, the therapist may approach the family and its members in a sequence determined, in part, by the principle of working with the primary resistance and by the affect evoked in the therapist by the family. For example, the parents of a 9-year-old boy whose symptoms suggested a borderline condition were convinced that their son had no emotional problems, and that any problems that he did have were caused by the school over the past 4 years. The mother, in strident contentious tones, excoriated the school in a paranoid manner while the father, in a schizoid mode, passively and intellectually agreed with his wife. In the second interview, the mother rushed into the office excitedly while the husband calmly positioned himself at a considerable distance from his wife and the therapist. She breathlessly revealed that she had had a dream the previous night and that a voice told her that her son did not have any emotional problems but had a *learning disability!* She immediately asked the therapist if he could treat her son's learning disabilities. Stifling a desire to explain to the parents that their son had severe emotional problems and that the mother's tense, overstimulating manner probably caused the difficulties, the therapist replied simply and in the affirmative. Attendant was a strong feeling of having been emotionally "muscled," compromised, and virtually stripped of one's identity as a therapist.

The mother was asked about her family. A frightened, angry look came over her face, but, managing a smile, she said, "I can't begin to tell you, it would be like opening Pandora's Box." The fear evoked in the therapist seemed related not only to her fear of becoming openly psychotic, but the therapist's fear of her decompensating. These important clues were used to establish the treatment plan wherein the parents agreed to send their son, Arthur, once a week and to come in themselves once or twice a month.

Arthur was bright, obsessive, and functioned in a passive–aggressive mode. For many weeks he kept me at a frustrating distance by talking about inanimate objects such as chemicals and rocks. We graduated to talking about plants, then about animals.

I respected and mirrored Arthur's distance while talking in a friendly interested manner. The topics appeared to be self-representations and were treated as such. Sessions with the parents were dominated by the mother's continued projective attacks on the school. On rare occasions, the parents complained about Arthur's behavior. In time, Arthur became the focus. His sessions changed dramatically as he brought in his pets. Finally, after bringing in a litter of kittens, Arthur brought in the mother cat. Commenting on the extreme fear, tenseness, and suspiciousness of the cat as well as revealing many "bad" qualities of the cat, Arthur's comments drew the therapist to create silently a parallel between the cat and the mother. The therapist then explored with Arthur the feasibility of "curing" the cat of her fears and "badness."

In sessions with the parents, frustration was evoked in the therapist by the distancing operations of the mother and father, consisting largely of angry tirades about virtually anything or anybody by the mother and silent consent by the father. In examining his feeling state, the therapist could imagine that Arthur had experienced fear, frustration, and anger at the parents' respective paranoia and schizoid withdrawal. At the same time, the therapist joined the parents' distancing maneuvers by remaining silent, joining in the attacks, and deliberately changing the topic when the parents began talking about themselves. The latter tactic seemed to stem the mother's suspicions.

Arthur continued to work at "curing" the mother cat. He was helped to fantasize about the causes of the cat's behavior as well as figuring out humane ways of helping her.

His behavior in school improved enough that the mother called the therapist to report that at a school conference she thought the teachers were talking about another boy at a different school. Arthur's progress was short-lived, for several weeks later the mother reported trouble in school and she said ominously, "I'm waiting for the other shoe to drop." The therapist requested the school to give reports of Arthur's misbehavior and withhold any signs of improvement. Arthur's behavior again improved over the course of several weeks after which the therapist received a frantic call from the mother complaining that her elder son was becoming increasingly withdrawn and that she wished a consultation. Apparently something went wrong in the subsequent consultation, for the parents did not pursue the matter. In retrospect, the therapist probably communicated that her elder son had an emotional problem rather than sharing with her the perplexity that she was experiencing. Perhaps the therapist manifested an untoward interest in treating the mother and father or communicated his fear of her psychosis. Although Arthur was treated successfully, the therapist could not treat other members of this family.

The sequence in this case was (a) resolution of the mother's resistance to treatment by joining her opinion about the diagnosis; (b) support of the mother's defenses against psychosis; (c) resolution of Arthur's schizoid defense; and (d) premature attempt to resolve the mother's resistance to her own treatment.

The Child as the Family Repository

Jeff, a 9-year-old, was referred through his school because of daydreaming, vast underachievement, and limited relatedness to his peers. The mother agreed to the referral because the boy was enuretic, and stubborn, which she felt was a strain in the relationship. I began work with Jeff who proved to be schizoid and peculiar. The only contact that I could make with him was through joining him in his bizarre solutions to common problems. There was little overall therapeutic contact and gain. I felt that I was dealing not only with his resistance but the family's resistance, and that the boy was the emotional repository for the family's problems.

In the meantime, the mother, who had had extensive analytic treatment, had come into "counseling" with a colleague. She had many borderline features and was barely sustaining herself in the family. She quickly left the child counseling relationship and requested individual psychotherapy. The whole family, as well as the individuals within it, were decompensating. The father, in particular, was demonstrating considerable pathology. To maintain the integrity of the marriage and the family, the mother's therapist spent considerable time showing the mother how to shore up her husband's defenses and prepare him for treatment.

After a year's work, Jeff said he wanted to suspend treatment because he had no more problems. After exploring his reasons for wanting to suspend treatment, I asked him how I should use his time after he left. He offered several ideas, each of which I explored but turned down. I finally asked him if he could find me someone who was as creative, friendly, agreeable, and inventive as he. He chuckled at my request, but I told him I was unwilling to discharge him until I found as nice a person as he. Within a week, I received a frantic phone call from Jeff's father imploring me to give him an appointment as soon as possible. When the father came in, he cried for half the session, indicating that he had been unable to work for several weeks (roughly coinciding with the weeks spent discussing suspension with Jeff), and that he wanted me to treat him. I told him I could not take on another member of the family and referred him to a colleague. Jeff's father's therapy has proceeded well.

Stubbornly holding to my position with Jeff about requiring a replacement for him, I soon received urgent requests from Jeff's parents that I treat another son who had suddenly developed depressive symptoms. After I saw him—one of the best motivated and hardest working boys I have seen—Jeff and I agreed to suspend our relationship. I keep using the word "suspend" because Jeff gave me the feeling that some day he would be back, most likely when the major pathology in the family had been resolved.

Everything was proceeding well in the individual treatment situation but from time to time Jeff's mother would call me expressing her concern about Jeff's behavior. In the meantime, the marital relationship was under severe strain in spite of the efforts of the spouses' therapists. I suggested that I would see Jeff's parents to teach them how to help Jeff. As I focused on Jeff, it became clear to the parents that the disagreements between them contributed heavily to Jeff's pathology. They requested help in creating a relationship that would help Jeff and their other children. As the marital problems became too much to handle, we would turn back to Jeff. In this instance, the father agreed to become the boy's therapist, and set up therapy sessions with the boy in the evening. When I respected the parents' need to avoid their problems and, as a defense, deal with their son, they eventually returned to their disagreements and conflicts.

Before the case could be successfully concluded, the father, who vigorously fought the transfer, was moved to another state by his firm. At that point, the second boy had been successfully treated and terminated, the parents had made plans to continue their individual treatment, and wished to reinitiate treatment for Jeff.

In this family, one therapist took on several therapeutic positions while working through the family's resistances: (a) he was Jeff's therapist; (b) he declined the role of Jeff's father's therapist; (c) he was marital therapist; (d) he was "supervisor" of the father's treatment of Jeff; and (e) he was Jeff's brother's therapist. One may ask many questions, "Isn't this too many roles?" "Weren't the transferences diluted or distorted?" "How could confidentiality be preserved?" The method certainly defies many principles of traditional therapy. Sequence therapy is experimental and needs verification across therapists and different types of cases.

A Family of Narcissists

Joe was a 13-year-old attractive boy whose mother was of Japanese ancestry and father was Caucasian. Joe's somewhat Oriental features were an unconscious source of discomfort for him in his upper-middle-class small town. To distract attention from his physical appearance, Joe would sport top hat, cane, occasionally a cape, and other quasibizarre items of dress. Although his unconventional father made little of Joe's appearance, the rest of the family was becoming not only ashamed of, but alarmed at, Joe's increasing preoccupation with antique and theatrical clothes. Joe was also referred for immature behavior and underachievement at school. Psychological testing revealed an intelligent nonpsychotic, egocentric boy.

After Joe and I made a contract wherein I was to help him conduct himself better in school, the sessions bogged down rather quickly. Joe could reveal relatively nothing about himself and his life, probably because of his intense feelings about his family history. I began to demonstrate interest in his clothing, particularly his hats. He had collected a few top hats and others usually of foreign style. When Joe indicated he had nothing on his mind, we talked incessantly about hats: where they could be bought, their manufacture, styles in different cultures, etc. When we seemed to run out of material about hats we talked of canes, capes, and boots. He would frequently bring in his clothing for discussion. During this period of 3–4 months no psychodynamic interpretation nor statements were made to Joe about his dress. My main task was to mirror obsessional interest in his hats, canes, and capes when he could not discuss his life. The reports from the parents during this period were that Joe slowly was giving up his accented dress. At one point when his parents asked Joe about me, he said in an exasperated tone, "All he wants to talk about is hats!" It seemed that as I swung more attention to clothing Joe behaviorally tilted away from his preoccupation and in the treatment sessions was able to turn to concerns about his self-esteem system, family, and peer relations.

Joe's mother, in the meantime, came into psychotherapy for help with some of her personal problems and her marriage. As her therapy progressed, there unfolded a picture of the father as a narcissistic character, absorbed in his artistic work, oblivious to the needs of his family, having extramarital interests, and dabbling in drugs. Gaining strength from her therapy, Mrs. M. began to make reasonable and appropriate demands of her husband. In his self-absorption, he could not begin to understand her needs, but did agree to come into treatment when she threatened separation. His entrance into therapy was made easier by the idea that he would be helping his son whose uniqueness he admired and fostered. As his narcissistic condition improved and his idealization of his son was analyzed, remarkable gains occurred in the lives of all of the family members, especially in that they identified themselves as a family and not only as unique, self-reliant mavericks.

The Symbiotic Mother–Child Dyad and Distant Father

Plagued by their 9-year-old's profound negativism and temper tantrums, Ted's parents sought consultation. Mrs. T. was an obsessive–compulsive woman whose need for order and control had driven Ted into his negative state to preserve his identity. She also had attempted to establish a symbiotic relationship with him, not only because of her own unresolved separation–individuation problem but because Mr. T. was an emotionally withdrawn man who was preoccupied primarily with his work.

Under the guise of being skeptical of the psychotherapeutic process and because she had been totally shut out of her son's previous therapy, Mrs. T. requested that she attend Ted's sessions. My impulse also was to shut her out. Recognizing the induced countertransference, and turning 180° from the counterresistance, I told her that with Ted's permission I would make her a co-therapist and teach her how to behave therapeutically with Ted. Her beaming protestations gave me a sense of melted resistances. My hunch about the countertransference proved correct for, later in the therapeutic process, Mrs. T. revealed that she had felt shut out of all relationships, primarily with her mother who constantly criticized and nagged her. She felt her father was disappointing and abandoning because he always agreed with his wife. I had the impression that any interpretation, confrontation, or discussion of Mrs. T.'s demand to enter her son's therapy would have driven them both out of treatment again. Rather, the invitation to make her a filial therapist frustrated her destructive wish to be rejected and created a symbiotic bond between us. I put myself in control, and set up a viable situation wherein I could study and treat the mother, child, and the symbiosis.

After several weeks of Ted testing the integrity of the therapist and the safety of the therapeutic situation with his mother present, Ted's intense negativism and belligerence modulated into more cooperative and pleasant behavior. Mrs. T. also reported that familial "uptightness" was lessening. Typically, we would discuss what made Ted have his "spasms." Threading through a maze of rationalizations for weeks, Ted began to focus on resentment about oral deprivations. Many of his statements and demands were outlandish such as "She never gets up in the morning to feed me . . . She always gives me the same junk for dinner." Actually, Mrs. T. was very devoted to rising early and preparing nutritious and varied meals for her family. I counseled her not to take the complaints personally, not to defend herself, but rather accept Ted's premise and explore with him why she has been such a "bad mother." Several individual and joint sessions with her husband were necessary at this point because Mrs. T., whose whole being revolved around "being a good mother," found Ted's complaints and accusations "too much to bear."

During these sessions, I worked on Mr. T.'s resistance to supporting his wife. Mr. T. came from a family where the father tyrannized the children through beatings and the mother was argumentative and controlling. It appeared that, without malevolence, he tended to drift away from interpersonal relations toward impersonal tasks. Mrs. T., in her romantic ideal, wanted her husband to help, love, and support her spontaneously. Pointing out that her husband's natural bent was away from people, I further examined her resistance to asking him for the emotional care that she needed. Again she returned to her early relationships with her family where one never asked, one just waited for attention, which seldom arrived.

Bolstered by these measures, Mrs. T. worked doggedly in the therapy sessions. While Ted was in the middle of a tirade about wanting only baloney for lunch and always wanting a certain kind of soup on the stove, Mrs. T. remembered that Ted's early infantile experience was marked by serious feeding problems. Apparently he could not ingest for months any fluids without regurgitation and projective vomiting. Once a milk substitute was found, the pediatrician put Ted on scheduled feedings that Ted's mother followed to the minute. The mother immediately began blaming herself in a self-destructive way. I asked her, "Why are you down on yourself, for after all weren't you being a good mother carrying out the instructions of an expert?" In individual and joint sessions we examined Mrs. T.'s depressive self-blaming mode more fully in terms of her being a loyal daughter who continued the criticisms and nagging of her mother on herself. That is, her mother made her feel that she deserved to be criticized, nagged, and yelled at. If Ted did not serve that function for her she provided it for herself. And if she wasn't busy getting it herself she could plague Ted or her husband.

A short period of working-through occurred wherein Ted greatly tempered his oral demands, Mrs. T. became less demanding of her self, and the father worked at relating himself more to his wife and son.

An Unstable Symbiosis in Adolescence

Mrs. M. requested a consultation for her 16-year-old daughter, Martha, who reportedly was doing poorly in school, was defiant at home, had periods of depression, was threatening to run away to Hollywood, and to become promiscuous. The joint interview revealed the mother to be moderately depressed, apparently about her daughter's behavior, but evidence pointed toward her depression as a function of being about to lose Martha who was the last child in a home where Mrs. M. was isolated from a work-oriented husband.

Martha refused to talk until her mother left the room. Then she revealed herself to be rather immature with unrealistic expectations of an acting career. However, she fully recognized the extent of her mother's depression and felt conflicted about leaving home. She wanted to be out of the house, independently pursuing her own career, but also felt quite responsible for the mother's welfare. Martha surmised that her mother needed her to be a baby, and would fall apart if she could not remain in the mothering role. Martha became convinced that the mother needed a baby. In exploring how the mother could have a baby, the therapist offered several suggestions such as the mother conceiving another child, adoption, getting another sibling, but Martha turned down each idea. The therapist, silently noting Martha's maturing sexuality yet regressive tie to the mother, suggested that Martha herself provide the mother with a baby. She brightened up and admitted sheepishly that she had been thinking a lot about becoming pregnant. Martha went on to reevaluate her plans about going to Hollywood immediately and talked about her responsibility to herself to complete her education and take acting lessons.

Although we made another appointment, Mrs. M. called to cancel several days later because Martha's condition and attitude had "vastly improved." The mother herself sounded less depressed and pessimistic apparently because Martha had decided not to abandon her.

A Schizophrenic Family

A 5-year-old boy was brought in because of disturbed reactions to kindergarten, encopresis and negativism. The parents offered no information about themselves and not only sidestepped personal questions, but also seemed offended and angry at probes. They dumped the boy on me and assumed minimal involvement in treatment. Their aloof yet controlling manner gave me a sense of being treated like a thing—a piece of shit. I imagined then how they treated their son and connected his symptoms with their attitude. Walter proved to be a mildly autistic boy whose inattentiveness and withdrawal were compounded by learning disabilities and a sad-eyed, drawn appearance. He was echolalic and had a profound disturbance in the ability to conceptualize and abstract with words.

As treatment proceeded with little involvement by the parents, the boy began to show some improvement which seemed to puzzle the mother since she had assumed that no change was possible. His change probably prompted her to join a group for mothers that the therapist was conducting. She made great strides in the group and chose to add an individual session. She terminated her son's treatment giving a financial rationale, that Walter was doing well, and that she really needed the treatment. Under this regime, Mrs. A. blossomed personally. She obtained a job that pleased her, became more sexually responsive, and generally became more alive and related. While she developed, she reported that her usually withdrawn husband had become agitated and paranoid particularly about her leaving the home for work and tennis. At one point he locked her out of the house and broke her sports equipment. Other evidence suggested that Mr. A.'s schizoid withdrawal was resolving into an active paranoid schizophrenia as a function of the changes in his son and wife. He also began to oppose her therapy vigorously. Focusing on the husband's behavior in her therapy sessions, she agreed to try to bring him in. After anticipating all of his objections to his being treated, she finally determined to ask him to come in to discuss how he could help her terminate the therapy. In the joint session, he acknowledged the need for his wife's changing. In the ensuing discussion of how she could best change, his highly intellectual, competitive, and omnipotent manner came to the fore when he announced the idea that *he* treat his wife. "After all, this therapy is just talk and I can talk to my wife as well as anyone." In the discussion of the therapeutic process he did allow that therapy had also to do with listening, *then* talking. Being a scholarly and scientific man, he would do some guided reading and accept supervision in his therapeutic endeavors with his wife while I phased out her treatment.

I noted Mr. A.'s unconscious passive–submissive homosexuality which was protected by his intellectual and challenging modes. The changes in his son and his wife had clearly upset the defensive equilibrium that he had established in his family. We agreed to meet biweekly, with his wife having the alternate week for her individual session. After several months, he proved to be an apt student and learned how to listen and reflect his wife's feelings during their "appointments," held virtually every evening. He was learning that an intimate heterosexual relationship could be satisfying. Mrs. A. seemed very pleased with her husband's understanding and attentiveness, and terminated with me with the feeling that she had lost a therapist but gained a husband. This arrangement stabilized the family for several years, at which time Mrs. A., with her husband's permission, came into treatment for a neurotic symptom.

In this schizophrenic family who basically treated each other primarily in anal terms, it seemed virtually impossible to gain access to their rigidly defended family and marital structure. Only through patient work with each member of the family over a period of years, using different therapeutic modalities, was the familial problem stabilized.

A Family Characterized by the Use of Projective Identification

In many instances, parents and children collaborate in a relationship wherein one or both parents experience the feelings of the child. As if trying to protect the child from experiencing unpleasantness associated with life, the parents seem to draw out, absorb, and act out the affect the child should be experiencing. This maneuver usually cripples the child and also may contribute to the loss of control or acting out of the child.

A late adolescent young man who had committed a serious crime seemed unconcerned about the consequences of his act. The prospect of jail, the conditions of parole, the deprivation of rights and freedom, loss of income, etc., were of minor import. On the other hand his father was near panic: he had lost weight, could not sleep, was developing somatic symptoms, and looked terrified. The mother sat quietly in a deep depression. As the family told their story and described the relationships, it appeared that, early in the boy's life, the action roles and responsibilities for experiencing emotion were established. As in the children's song of "Farmer in the Dell," the father took the anxiety and the wife took the depression, while the child, like an empty barrel, bumped and careened through life. From the history I could not substantiate a hypothesis about a "superego lacunae." That is, the parents did not unconsciously encourage or enjoy their son's action-oriented life. Rather, they took on his anxiety, guilt, shame, and depression according to their respective characterologic dispositions.

I noted the son's thin smile when the father was bemoaning the son's fate.

T: John, what are you pleased about?
J: Nothing.
T: Something must have pleased you because as your father was describing how worried he was about you, you were smiling. I was wondering whether you were pleased that he's so concerned and worried about you.
J: *(Shrug.)* I don't know. Maybe.
T: Mr. J., how long have you been worried about John?
Mr. J: Ever since he could walk and run.
T: John, did you know that your Dad has been worried so much about you for such a long time?
J: Yeh, but he overdoes it.

When I asked for an explanation, John scornfully cited many examples of his father's worrisome nature.

T: Well, John, would you like your father to worry less or would you like to help him to live longer because it seems that his worry is affecting his heart?
J: Sure.
T: Mr. J., would you like to worry less?
Mr. J: Sure.
T: I have a plan. John, your father has deprived you of your right to worry and he has taken on himself all the

> worries of the family. He's like a magnet for worries or even like a worry sponge because he absorbs all the worries of the family and keeps them inside which ruins him. So if you want to relieve him of this terrible burden he has taken on himself all you have to do is start worrying yourself. And the other part is that your Dad has to stop worrying so much about you. Furthermore, he has to teach you how to worry. I suggest that once a day you and your dad sit down and discuss the amount and kind of worry each of you are shouldering and how it should be distributed. If there's any disagreement your Mom can be brought in to referee.

At the next week's session, the father had lost his hunted look and lines had disappeared from his face. He was notably calmer. His wife remarked that he looked and acted 10 years younger. John and his father had talked almost everyday about the distribution of worry and about other aspects of their lives.

In a subsequent session, I worked in a similar manner with John and his mother about her assuming the responsibility of absorbing all of the depressive emotions in the family.

Within several weeks of family sessions alternating with John's individual sessions, John's blandness, cockiness, and provocativeness—especially with authority figures—faded into an overt concern about his future and a willingness to cooperate. In an authentic manner, he impressed the judge and justice personnel with his determination to become a good citizen so that the impending serious sentence was suspended. Shortly thereafter, John, in spite of his record, found himself a responsible position that he maintained.

Chapter 8

FAILURE-INDUCING PATIENTS AND FAMILIES

In any psychotherapeutic endeavor, the therapeutic process rarely proceeds at a maximally efficient rate, especially with more primitively organized patients and families. There are, of course, situations with no progress, failure of therapeutic effort, and even regression. Chessick (1971) and Wolman (1972) have courageously addressed themselves to this issue. I consider that the patient and family are *not* at fault when failure occurs. Rather, any failure to reach a goal is largely due to the therapist's functioning. This message can be communicated fairly early in treatment when patients complain of lack of progress and, in particular, when patients excessively blame themselves for the stalemate. When the patient asks for treatment and the therapist and patient agree to the goals and conditions, the therapist is basically responsible for the treatment. Suppose patients do not meet their part of the agreement, such as not appearing for sessions, coming late, not paying attention, or not talking. The therapist must analyze and resolve the resistances. Furthermore, it is the therapist's task to investigate his or her own countertransferences and counterresistances to meeting therapeutic goals. For example, in an initial interview with an extremely attractive young woman whose marriage was failing, a therapist found himself seriously considering whether he could treat a woman who was so fascinating to him. When she called to cancel her next appointment, he knew by his sense of relief that she had surmised his inner turmoil and had not been willing to chance the relationship.

Another kind of countertransference–counterresistance is having one or more patients who are like emotional albatrosses around one's neck. Some therapists tend to have one or more patients who consistently telephone at odd hours, threaten suicide, intimidate the therapist, or otherwise are worrisome and annoying.

Other therapists seem to have a penchant for maintaining one or more patients who are in various states of "emergencies," who "require" hospitalization, who "need" medication, or "must" talk to the therapist on the telephone. These therapists may certainly be treating very disturbed patients, but they help the therapist maintain a certain equilibrium or personal norm that also characterizes other aspects of his or her personal and social life.

Therapists are especially vulnerable to countertransference reactions when personal stresses such as divorce, familial illness, or death occur. The countertransferences are not created anew, but usually are exacerbated reactions to latent or character trends. For example, one therapist whose hostility to women usually emerged in the form of frustrating seductiveness and extramarital affairs was prompted to proceed with a divorce. Being an unusually perceptive therapist, he noted, but could not control, an urge to blame his women patients for their seductiveness, their lack of movement in treatment, and especially to excoriate mothers who failed to take loving care of their children.

Another therapist who was in a supervisory–therapeutic relationship with me complained that, in spite of her best conscious intentions to her fiancé, he took offense at her overtures and in general "blamed" her for everything. I noted that a similar dynamic was occurring in her treatment of patients. Although she was a devoted and conscientious therapist, her patients did not take kindly to her confrontations and interpretations. In a counterresistant turn she tended to lecture them about resistance and blame them for not getting well. Having completed an analysis, she immediately recalled her own untolerable sense of blame induced by her unyieldingly critical parents, as well as her own self-blame in not helping them in their illness.

Some therapists actively avoid contacts with parents and families, usually out of a rejection of their own parents. Others stimulate excessive contact with parents and families as if they are trying to recreate ideal families for themselves. Family therapists sometimes rigidly insist on family therapy in all cases. I have had a number of parents and children who had felt coerced into family therapy and challenged to talk prematurely about submerged feelings. Frequently these families *do* need family therapy as a matter of choice, but they must go through other processes before being able to use and benefit from family therapy. For example, one family desperately needed a scapegoat to protect themselves against talking about the serious illness of the mother. Rejecting a therapist who insisted on family therapy, they prevailed upon me to see their "lying and deceiving son." After a few individual sessions, the parents were pleased to come in and talk about the family "secret." Waters (1976) has discussed the use of family as a defense against examining the marital relationship.

Other therapists subject to countertransference–resistance difficulties are those graduated from and certified by psychoanalytic institutes that provide substantial training in adult therapy. Many graduates maintain their practice within the confines of their training. Others assume that their psychoanalytic training with adults prepares them for treatment of children, adolescents, groups, families, and marital problems. Many are truly gifted in dealing with almost any human problem while others need training and supervision in specialized modes of treatment in order to conduct creditable therapy.

The therapist trained in the treatment of neuroses and who is heavily influenced by psychoanalytic theory and techniques of the neurosis is poorly equipped to deal with prevalent borderline and narcissistic disorders. Fortunately, more attention in the institutes and literature has been directed to the treatment of the borderline and psychotic conditions so that fewer therapists are likely to function with lacunae.

Some treatment failures remain totally bewildering. The termination frequently is not discussed, not planned for, nor anticipated. In retrospect and too late, one sees that as a matter of style, the family or parents leave in their trail a series of frustrated and bewildered people whose reaction is "What did I do to deserve this?" Any attempt to reinstate treatment is met with evasion, deceit, or stone-walling. These families can be detected because the presenting problem is usually a child who acts in a bewildered and/or abusive manner and the parents themselves appear to be very naïve and seemingly eager to receive help. When these families are retained for treatment, the therapist finds out the source of the bewilderment pattern and their unconscious intent to bewilder others. Because of their seeming naiveté and cooperation, these families tend to appeal to the omniscience and omnipotence of some therapists. It seems far better to plead ignorance about the therapeutic situation and join the family in their bewilderment.

A similar type of family that is easy to lose in the course of treatment is the family that induces errors. In a clinic situation, the secretary takes the wrong phone number, or the initial interview time is misunderstood, or requested records never arrive. While everything seems to go wrong, the source of errors is obscure. Any implication that the family is somehow responsible for the misunderstanding is a grave error because the family is hostilely defensive, very frightened, and will terminate treatment. It is best to take responsibility for errors, for these families tend to come from backgrounds where they felt they could never do anything right. When they find someone who will not reject their massive projective identifications, they are secretly delighted and will remain with the therapist. At the same time, the therapist must be ready to analyze and handle the enormous hostility in all the family members. For example, this type of family may be asked questions such as "Why do you think *I* (or the secretary) made the mistake?" Their answer will provide clues to understanding why *they* function incorrectly. A question such as "What can *I* do to avoid making mistakes in the future?" may evoke an answer providing a therapeutic avenue to resolving *their* characterologic fault.

Finally, there appear to be patients whose only reason for living is to prove that the other person is a failure. In proving that the therapist is a failure, the massive defense of projection is apparent in virtually every domain of their lives. These are usually preoedipal patients who have been subjected to and have introjected massive criticism and blame and hostility from the parent(s). Instead of developing feelings and values of their own, they function more out of the feelings of the parent(s). The projections and ability to blame others actually are a life-saving device which, if not held in place, might develop into attacks on the self. These persons seem to have an uncanny ability to induce profound feelings of guilt, blame, and worthlessness in others. The therapist must acknowledge these induced and evoked feelings and understand their source. If the therapist is successful in the treatment, the patient usually confesses later that it was their intent to make the therapist suffer, never to compliment the therapist, and otherwise to defeat—if not destroy—the therapist. I suspect, however, that many therapists do not acknowledge the induced feelings of failure but defensively process those feelings, thus promoting therapeutic failure.

Another variant of these failure-inducing patients is the disposition to portray themselves as completely helpless, hopeless, and incurable. They have an uncanny knack for evoking in the therapists profound feelings of impotence and failure even though they do not directly attack the therapist. Many therapists cannot bear to see their patients verbalize such feelings and may act on their own sense of failure by yielding to pleas for medication or hospitalization. In some instances, therapists themselves suggest or go along with such drastic tactics that provide the dénouement for therapy.

Novick (1980) attributes a *negative therapeutic motivation* to these patients. He hypothesizes that the resolve to fail and defeat the therapist develops before the patient enters therapy. The negative therapeutic motivation occurs not only in children and adolescents but in parents who take every opportunity to defame therapists for "their" failure. Any sign of progress is vigorously denied or, if acknowledged, is not attributed to the therapist's efforts. Another source of negative therapeutic motivation, according to Novick, resides in the referral source who, usually subjected to failure by the patient, wishes to share ignominy with a colleague. Novick suggests that therapists look to their countertransferential omnipotence fantasies. In the event of a degree of failure, Novick communicates to the patient that all is not lost and that failure can lead to growth and development.

Chapter 9

COUNTERTRANSFERENCE IN THE PSYCHOTHERAPY OF CHILDREN AND ADOLESCENTS

The Literature

According to Freud, the most difficult and time-consuming work of therapy lies in the resolution of resistances. Because one of the greatest sources of difficulty in handling resistances arises from within the therapist—the countertransference and the counterresistance—the therapist's countertransferences must be well known and used to therapeutic advantage, especially in the treatment of children, adolescents, and their families.

The Dearth of Literature

A most significant feature in the area of countertransference toward children and adolescents had been the limited literature. Of 217 references on countertransference provided by an American Psychology Association Abstract Search covering 1967 to 1976, only 10 references—six of which were foreign sources—pertained to children or adolescents. *The Bibliography for Training in Child Psychiatry* (Berlin, 1976) has 19 references. The venerable *Psychoanalytic Study of the Child* provides 10 index entries in 25 years. The three editions of the *Index of Psychoanalytic Writings* (Grinstein, 1975) cite only 17 references from 1900 to 1969. A scan of subject indexes in child therapy books reveals only nominal attention to countertransference.

Several authors also have noted the relative lack of attention to countertransference. Maurice Green (1972) speaks of the "neglect," as do Christ (1964) and Akaret and Stockhamer (1965) in reference to late adolescents.

Similarly, in case conferences and reports, attention has traditionally been on topics other than the therapist's feelings.

The Neglect as a Reflection of Countertransference Problems

Kohrman et al. (1971) also recognize that "we don't talk about such things," but provide an excellent analysis of the lacuna. Taking an historical and cultural tack, they argue that the first child analysts had been educators who dealt with children from lower socioeconomic groups. Functioning out of an educational mode, the educator–analysts emphasized needs for growth through learning, sheltering, protecting, and transmitting of cultural values. The therapists' backgrounds oriented them to function as real objects, to develop a positive transference, and provide a "giving" relationship. Aichhorn (1935, 1964) is a good example of an early worker who functioned as educator and psychoanalyst, as is Berta Bornstein, who had worked as Fürsorgerin (combining some duties of social and welfare worker), according to Blos (1974).

Another factor that may have deflected the early child therapists from developing the concept of countertransference was Anna Freud's (1926[1927b]) declaration that "transference neurosis" could not be established with children although she allowed that "transference reactions" could occur (p. 44). Forty years later, she (1965) revised her position by recognizing that "transference neurosis" could occur, but not equal to the adult variety in every respect (p. 36). Abbate (1964), Van Dam (1966), and Casuso (1963) provide important panel reports on this issue.

Anna Freud (1955) also stated that: ". . . negative impulses toward the analyst . . . are essentially inconvenient, and should be dealt with as soon as possible. The really fruitful work always takes place with a positive attachment." (p. 41) This pronouncement may have led to an inculcation of guilt and anxiety in therapists who found their charges to hold less than a "positive attachment." And, the curious disregard of countertransference phenomena by Anna Freud and by Melanie Klein probably deterred less courageous therapists from formal exploration.

Obstacle or Instrument

In adult psychoanalysis, the change from viewing countertransference as an obstacle to using it as a formidable vehicle has been traced by Feiner (1979), Issacharoff (1979), and Epstein (1979). The field of child therapy has not shown the same steady course toward a studied use of countertransference. Among child analysts, Bornstein (1948) appears to be the first to delineate some of the factors that *limit* a therapist's effectiveness. She cited children's unpredictability, their highly charged affects, narcissism, and the closeness of their productions to the unconscious. Lebovici (1951), Lebovici et al. (1970a & b) were early and continuing contributors to the understanding of the *pitfalls* of countertransference not only to the child, but to the parents. Slavson (1952) tended to see countertransference problems in terms of personality types of the therapist. For example, he depicted "negative" therapists whose anger and disapproval was a function of their identification with their own parents' attitudes toward them and a rejection of their childhood. Kut Rosenfeld and Sprince (1965) note the "lack of self-assurance" that influences the therapists' handling of borderline children. The physical attacks and the denial of the therapist's existence "must be tolerated" (p. 514).

Szurek (1950) saw identification with the child as promoting acting out. Rubenstein and Levitt (1957) warned of the therapist's feelings toward the father of the child. Corday (1967) spelled out the dangers of the countertransference for a male therapist treating pubertal girls. Recently Pearson (1968), Friend (1972), and Masterson (1972) have recognized the importance of the countertransference, but tend still to portray it as an obstacle to be surmounted by supervision or personal analysis. Marshall (1978) found countertransference to be the central problem in the treatment of delinquents, especially since contacts with family, school, and court may be necessary.

Viewing countertransference in a more utilitarian vein, Colm (1955) appears to be the first to suggest that countertransference is a necessary means of investigating the interpersonal field. Winnicott (1958) opened wider the range of affects that could be talked about in detail and in a personal manner. Proctor (1959) spelled out both the pitfalls and the uses of countertransference reactions in the treatment of juveniles with character disorders.

Holmes (1964) sensitively discussed the active use of induced feelings in the treatment of adolescents, while Christ (1964) candidly described his sexual transference–countertransference with a psychotic girl, emphasizing the private and personal nature of his feelings rather than the pathological. Kohrman et al. (1971) provide a well-balanced discussion of the active use and dangers of countertransference phenomena. Strean's (1970) book also provides a more positive view of countertransference. Marshall (1976) suggests that countertransference feelings provide clues to the analysis of the resistance of children and adolescents. Giovacchini (1974), in noting that recovery of infantile memories and traumatic childhood events are rare today, believes "that these transference–countertransference reactions, if properly handled, become an event that is equivalent to lifting infantile amnesia" (p. 282). Marcus (1980) sees countertransference from two points of view: (a) reactions generated by the developmental level of the child, i.e., symbiotic, latency; (b) reactions generated by the different phases of therapy: beginning, termination, etc.

"There's too much of it"

Many authors subscribe to the "there's too much of it" theory, which provides a paradoxical explanation for the neglect of countertransference. It appears that overwhelming feelings of guilt, inadequacy, and anxiety underlie many therapists' attitudes toward their child and adolescent patients, particularly those therapists whose analyses and supervision have not fully encompassed the personal and technical problems of conducting therapy with troubled young people. King (1976) cites rejection, the wish to punish, and appeasement–identification as three significant countertransference reactions of child care workers to violent young people. Giovacchini (1975) cites procrastination of adolescents as being particularly trying. Pichon-Rivière (1952) discusses competition with the mother, stealing the child from the mother, and pregnancy envy.

Frequently, therapists working with children in institutional settings are extremely reticent in revealing their feelings toward their charges, and are loath to comment on their methods. For example, in one setting, only after some trust was established were those workers able to reveal their bewilderment and deep despair in handling their patients and to allude to the guilt about their feelings and practices. In one instance, a highly popular group worker, who was being promoted, did not attend the farewell meeting of his group because he could not handle their positive feelings. More frequently, fear and anger were the dominant confusing feelings.

In general, the earliest literature on countertransference emerged from work with schizophrenic children in institutions. This certainly is no coincidence, for it seems fair to say that the more primitively organized the patient, the greater the affective impact on the therapist. Moreover, sparked by the child, the interpersonal relationships among staff, administration, and families are at a high level of tension, usually of a countertransferential nature. Shermo et al. (1949) noted that the unresolved conflict among staff increased the acting out and destructive group formations in a psychiatric ward. Ekstein's group has been especially aware of countertransferential problems in individual and milieu therapy. For example, they (1959) discuss not only the therapist's countertransference to an institutionalized child, but emphasize the staff's countertransference as a compounding disturbing factor. Marshall (1978) provides a clinical portrait of a milieu therapy program where a team of child workers tended to use reality problems as a defense against examining countertransference issues. He hypothesizes that the ability to discuss countertransference represented the acme of the functioning of the total program. In a paper that should be read by all child therapists, Bettleheim (1975) describes the personal reactions of the workers in his milieu therapy program.

Bornstein (1948) illustrates the threat and fear that grip the therapist because of the child's emotional lability and easy availability of libidinal and aggressive material. She cites the seductiveness and provocativeness of children which facilitate the acting out of the therapist, and warned of the danger of regression, which "no one in continuous contact with children can escape." Kabcenell (1974) amplifies Bornstein's position. Bick (1962) believes that the stresses and strains produced in the child analyst

> . . . are more severe than those on the analyst of adults. The intensity of the child's dependence on his positive and negative transference, the primitive nature of his fantasies, tend to arouse the analyst's own unconscious anxieties. The violent and concrete projections of the child into the analyst may be difficult to contain. Also, the child's suffering tends to evoke the analyst's parental feelings, which have to be controlled so that the proper analytic role can be maintained. All these problems tend to obscure the analyst's understanding and to increase in turn his anxiety and guilt about his work. (p. 330)

Friend (1972) views the countertransference as evidence of residual pathology

> . . . opportunities to defend against the incompletely analyzed infantile–parental problems of the analyst, the omnipotent need to maintain a nurturing feminine identification or a powerful, authoritative masculine identification with the adolescent as a figure for projective identification. There may be unconscious seductive erotic determinants of unresolved infantile components and a desire for leadership or omnipotence that extends the analyst into areas of interaction that he himself would never individually narcissistically enjoy. The painfulness of an individual's adolescent reactions may temper the unconscious aspect of one's own reactions and substitute for unresolved aspects of this developmental phase. (p. 325)

Friend also cites the "complexity, strain, and communication problem" (p. 327) in exclusively treating children "just as a mother might have too many children to take care of personally." (p. 328) Bettleheim (1975) in a poignant statement about his therapists, believes that to work successfully with their patients they need "an infinitely higher level of personal integration than is necessary" (p. 259).

Formidable defenses are erected against destructive thoughts, impulses, and feelings toward children. One of our cultural values is that of helping and loving children. Child abuse is considered an abomination. While respect and care for children are signs of civilized life, the recorded history of the child offender (Sanders, 1970) and of children in general (DeMause, 1974a & b) indicates that children have been treated with incredible savagery. Reingold (1967) believes that impulses toward infanticide are more widespread than commonly accepted. Virtually every mother who has been in treatment with me has guiltily expressed a wish to be rid of her children in one way or another. Moreover, patients frequently report that their parents wanted to be rid of them. Winnicott (1958) gives 18 reasons why a mother may hate her children, both boys and girls. Although the treatment of violent children has been described frequently, very little (King, 1976) has been written about the feelings of the therapist. Marshall (1974,1978) has outlined a theory and technique of handling the delinquent and aggressive child through a utilization of the therapist's feelings. Masterson (1972) refers to this area tangentially. The relative silence in this countertransferential area suggests that "there is too much of it" and that the violent feelings of the therapist are perhaps not being used constructively, let alone recognized.

Closely associated with the firm taboos against aggression toward children and infanticide are the strictures against sexuality. DeMause (1974a & b) presents some startling reports of child sexual abuse and adds that historic reports of sexual abuse of children are still locked in library vaults.

The Homuncular Theory

Another factor, which may be termed the "homuncular" or "little adult" theory, was suggested by a young therapist who, when asked about his reasons for wanting to treat children, jokingly replied, "Kleine kinder, kleine tsores; gröesse kinder, gröesse tsores" (little children, little problems; big children, big problems). The primitive, fallacious, and lulling assumption is that the type and intensity of countertransference problems with children are more diminutive than with adults. This "little adult" theory may reflect a denial defense against the contrary—"there's too much of it."

Contribution of Client-Centered Therapy

Another source of neglect of countertransference may stem from the popularity of the client-centered approach to psychotherapy. Child therapists such as Axline and Moustakas emphasized the need for unconditional acceptance of their client's feelings. This acceptance and the correlative permissiveness seeped into the sphere of behavior. Moustakas (1953), for example, advocated telling his child patients, "In here you are free to do what you want." Yet the notion of "setting limits" certainly had to evolve in order to contain intolerable behavior. Dorfman (1951) indicated that, in order to remain emotionally accepting, client-centered therapists set limits including terminating the session and putting the child out of the playroom. Truax and Carkhuff (1967) provide evidence that successful therapists had accurate empathic understanding, nonpossessive warmth, and genuineness. However, one gets the impression that feelings other than these are not permissible, and lead to negative therapeutic consequences. Therefore they are indicative of an unsuccessful therapist and must be eliminated. They write

> . . . counselors or therapists who are low in communicated accurate empathy, nonpossessive warmth and genuineness are ineffective and produce negative or deteriorative change in the patient because they are noxious stimuli who serve primarily as aversive reinforcers *and* also because they elicit negative affect in the patient which increases the level of the patient's negative self-reinforcement, increases the level of negative affect communicated to others, and thus increases reciprocally the negative affect and negative reinforcement received from others. (pp. 161–162)

Jourard (1971) has suggested that disclosing the therapist's feelings to the patient and working the feelings into the relationship are valid options.

The Parental Trap

Still another source of avoidance of countertransferential feelings may be rooted in the fact that most therapists are parents themselves and tend to see their own children in their patients. The feelings, both positive and negative, that should ordinarily remain in the background, filter into the consultation and playroom so that transferences and countertransferences are evolved but not explored.

The Nature of the Model

A medical model of disease seems to be a major conceptual view of countertransference. Preventively, it is as if one must go through an elaborate process of immunization so as not to experience any of the dread symptoms. If one should develop any of its symptoms, one should go for treatment. A less threatening medical model might view the countertransference as normal growth and development that the patient induces in the therapist. This accretion would represent a regeneration of pathology from the patient's past. Colm (1955) uses a field theory–interpersonal model that conceptualizes countertransference as a *necessary* dynamic part of the interpersonal field. Its presence provides the therapist with an opportunity to help the patient. A communications model would be less anxiety-evoking in therapists, as suggested by Searles (1975) and Langs (1975), where the feelings of the therapist may reflect unconsciously transmitted messages of the patient. Kramer and Byerly (1978) suggest that increasing experience and success in the treatment of children diminish untoward emotional reactions to child and parent.

The Contribution of Behavior Therapy

Historically, the last resistance to exploring countertransference evolves from the behavior therapy movement. Although there has been much research on "therapist variables," there appears to be little interest in investigating feeling states of the therapist. There have been important exceptions such as Bandura (1956) who found a positive correlation between therapist anxiety and competence. Bandura et al. (1960) examined the therapist's "approach-avoidance" reactions to patient hostility. Conceptually, there appears to be little room for such a subjective variable as countertransference. When therapist attitudes do seem to interfere with patient progress, the behavior therapists seem to "rise above it" and recommend further training—which brings us back to Freud's original position.

The Definitions

The reader is referred to Epstein and Feiner's (1979) edited book, *Countertransference,* for discussions of definitions of countertransference. The material presented here focuses on issues pertaining primarily to children, adolescents and parents.

While the term can be used generically to describe all therapists' reactions to their patients, countertransference, in this sense, becomes too vague and general to be of help. A. Reich (1960) pointed out that this "totalistic" definition, preferred by many, is of limited value, just as useless as defining transference as the total reaction of the patient to the therapist. A "totalistic" definition, however, does have the virtue of removing some of the stigma from "being in countertransference."

Maenchen (1970) considers countertransference an overworked and meaningless term if it is used to cover all of the analyst's feelings and actions. She wishes to use the term only to describe the analyst's use of the child as a transference object. Kramer and Byerly (1978) essentially agree but extend the concept to the analyst's reactions to the parents. Bernstein and Glenn (1978) in a perspicacious discussion, adhere to a "narrow" definition of countertransference according to Freud's idea that countertransference is an unconscious reaction to the patient's transference.

However, Bernstein and Glenn go on to describe the following emotional reactions in the analyst:

1. *Transference reactions* occur when the therapist "is not reacting to the patient's transference. For instance, he may have transference reactions to his patient's appearance or behavior." (p. 376). Generalized characterologic transference reactions are also noted such as rigidified stances to all patients as paternal or sibling rivals.
2. *Identification* with the child with a concomitant transference to the child's parents.
3. *Counteridentification* occurs when analysts, in reaction to the child's identification with them, mirror the child's identification and both fall into a regressed undifferentiated state.
4. *Experiencing the patient as an extension of oneself* may also lead to fusion states.
5. *Reactive identification* occurs in the form of the analyst acting to the child in a manner opposite to that of the parents.
6. *Reactions to the patient as a real person* which include sympathy, signal affects, and a failure to empathize because of differences in developmental levels.

They argue that there are analysts "who injudiciously welcome overt countertransference manifestations as clues to the patient's neurosis." Furthermore, they take issue with the proposition that patients induce responses in the analyst through projective identification. Finally, they state, "Those who praise counter-transference confuse this phenomenon with empathy and signal affects" (p. 378).

Kohrman et al. (1971) prefer the use of "counterreaction" as a generic term for emotional reactions of the therapist and reserve "countertransference proper" for the therapist's spontaneous, unconscious reaction to the patient's transference. They also recognize a "universal countertransference" that is the total response of the child analyst to the total therapeutic situation. A third counterreaction is considered to be "transference," which is a "spontaneous, unconscious, conflictful and immaturely determined reaction to the patient as he really is" (p. 491). It is a reaction to a specific patient and not a generalized or characteristic attitude to all patients.

Christ (1964), from his experience in treating psychotic children and adolescents, emphasizes the therapist's defense against pregenital impulses as a major part of the countertransference reaction. When these impulses are "recognized and not unconsciously defended against or acted on, they include some of the therapist's main tools in understanding his patient. These are the foundations on which empathy and insight are built. (p. 332)

Eight Types of Countertransference

To be more precise and operational, three broad dimensions of countertransference can be discerned that yield eight types. One dimension depends on the source of the countertransference: therapist or patient. That is, one subtype of countertransference is that response of the therapist whose source is the patient and his or her behavior. It is a response that most therapists would experience in a given situation and is similar to Winnicott's (1958) "objective countertransference" which is "the analyst's love and hate in reaction to the actual personality and behavior of the patient." (p. 195) The objective countertransference derives from the projective identification of the patient and is an emotional, nonverbal, unconscious communication to the therapist as Searles (1975) has described. Freud's (1913) concept of countertransference and his notion of resistance as communication are consonant with this type of countertransference.

Another subtype of countertransference is that response of the therapist whose source is the *internal promptings of the therapist.* This subtype, akin to a true transference reaction or neurosis has been termed "subjective countertransference" by Spotnitz (1969).

There is another dimension to this definition: the degree of consciousness. On one side of this continuum there is no recognition of a reaction to the patient, while on the opposite pole the therapist is fully aware of any reactions and can determine from where the main stimulus derives.

From a theoretic and clinical point of view, a third dimension may be added, that of specificity–generality. Some countertransference reactions are specific to a particular patient or perhaps type of patient whereas other countertransference reactions oc-

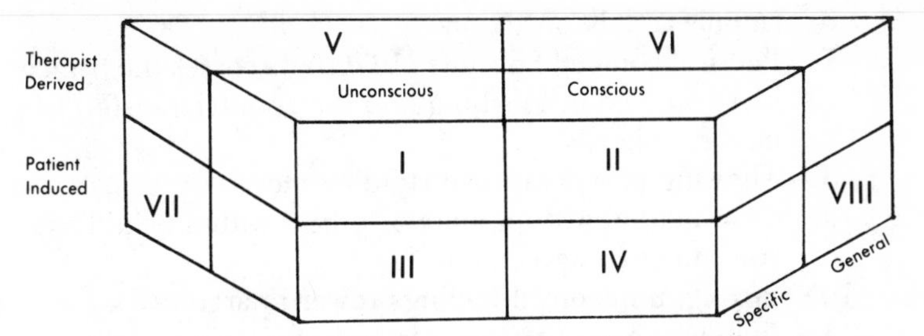

Figure 9–1 Dimensions and types of countertransferences

cur with all patients under all conditions. Types I through IV (Figure 9–1) countertransferences refer to specific and unique situations and constellations. Types V through VIII countertransferences pertain to characterological and stylistic trends more deeply entrenched in the therapist's personality, and suggest character types who are potentially noxious to patients.

Traditionally, the unconscious–therapist derived response (Type I) has been the major and most feared type of countertransference, and is a true transferential response to the patient —a whole response (Gitelson, 1952), posing a symbiotic problem (Tower, 1956). The resolution of a Type I countertransference appears to require additional analysis and/or analytically oriented supervision. The major problem is that the therapist, because of the unconscious nature of the conflict, is unaware of the real situation. The therapist acts out in concert with the patient, and can be alerted only through recognition signs such as those spelled out by Menninger (1958), Cohen (1952), and Spotnitz (1969). Other clues, applicable to children and adolescents, are:

1. Excessive play with diminution of talk
2. Quick yielding to requests
3. Gratification of child, particularly feeding and gift-giving
4. Any strong feeling, especially accompanied by guilt or anxiety
5. "Lulling" (Sarnoff, 1976) "The process of altering attention . . . when a child plays out similar fantasies repetitively" (pp. 243–246)

6. Impulsive talk or action
7. Physical contact; Spotnitz (1976b) discusses the principles involved in touching and the countertransference implications
8. Allowing parents to use child's time
9. Consultation with parents or others without child's involvement or agreement
10. Strong, unresolved feelings toward parents
11. Inability to involve parents appropriately
12. Preoccupation with changing behavior especially as desired by parents or school. Ekstein (1978) warns of "becoming enmeshed with parental and environmental interventions" (p. 458)
13. Idealization by child and/or parents (Greenacre, 1966)
14. Fantasies of rescuing the child from "bad parents" (Sterba, 1940). Historically, this sign, along with identification with the child (Szurek, 1950), constitute the first observations of countertransference. Although these phenomena are commonplace and certainly can lead to treatment problems, they have been overworked and too frequently used as cudgels by child therapy supervisors

Some of these factors, when under conscious control, may be used as parameters.

In the treatment of children where the situation is more labile and where the child tolerates errors, Type I countertransference may occur for longer periods than with adults. A reflection of Type I countertransference can be found in the quality of the relationship with the youth's parents. If the therapist has too little or too much contact with the parents, or if the therapist/counselor of the parents experiences difficulty, the therapist may search for Type I countertransference. If the therapist is in the Type I countertransference for any period of time, further personal analysis is recommended.

Type II countertransference (conscious–therapist derived) is less pernicious, but may be troublesome to resolve. In this situation the therapist "knows" the problem, but cannot surmount it. Analytically oriented supervision is indicated.

Type III countertransference usually stagnates or obscures the therapeutic situation. Although much may seem to go on in the session, no real movement occurs because the patient is in control of the treatment. Strean (1970), Langs (1975), and Searles (1975) address themselves to this area. Supervision of any kind, including peer discussion, can be helpful. Frequently, Type III resolves into Type IV countertransference.

Type IV countertransference, which is the focus of the clinical material in this chapter, denotes that the patient is primarily responsible for inducing thoughts and feelings (but not action) in the therapist that are fully within the therapist's awareness and grasp.

Types III and IV are akin to projective identification wherein the patient projects *into* the therapist's cognitive, affective, and motor systems—those split-off elements of his or her functioning. The therapist then may think, feel, and even act as if he or she were the patient, or controlled by the patient. Langs (1976) sees projective identification as an "interactional effort to put one's own inner contents into someone else, in order to manage these inner contents externally and to possibly benefit from the effects at management undertaken by the other person" (p. 26).

On the patient's side, this process is unconscious. In Type III countertransference the therapist, while thinking, feeling, and acting as the patient, has no awareness of the impact of the patient. In Type IV countertransference, the therapist readily understands the nature of his or her own feeling state, recognizes the source, and prepares an intervention based on a comprehension of the total situation.

The therapist's main task is to study the interactional field and devise proper interventions. There is considerable support for the idea that Type IV countertransference is not only unavoidable, but is also a prerequisite to successful therapy, especially with those patients who function primarily at primitive levels. For example, Spitz (1956) comments on three steps by which the analyst understands the patient.

1. The therapist becoming aware of the derivatives of his or her own unconscious response to the patient's unconscious

2. Inferring of the underlying processes in himself or herself
3. Creating a transitory identification with the patient

Ackerman (1959) believes that avoidance of countertransference may protect the therapist but will not heal the patient. Langs (1980) differentiates on a continuum between *"preponderant"* countertransferences, which constitute a major disruptive input into the therapeutic interaction, and *"inevitable"* countertransferences, which stem from the inherent "limitations of the therapist's own therapy and self-analysis, and in his condition as a human being" (p. 381). Langs then argues that the inevitable countertransferences can be used in the service of curing not only the patient but also the therapist.

Ekstein (1978) notes,

> The peculiar nature of the psychotic transference is paralleled by its peculiar countertransference potential with both positive and negative aspects. If they can be used properly, they can lead to successful treatment; an error can result in interruption and disruption. (p. 457)

While most analysts warn about the inadvisability of being pulled into a countertransference, Ekstein warns against resisting being drawn into the psychotic process. He notes that therapists defend themselves by becoming "educator[s]" and "attempt[s] to confront the patient with reality, to reeducate him, to seek adjustments, thus avoiding the resolution of inner struggle which involved primary process" (p. 457).

Annie Reich (1951) offers this aphorism, "Countertransference is a necessary prerequisite of analysis. If it does not exist, the necessary talent and interest is lacking" (p. 30).

Type V Generalized, unconscious, therapist-derived reactions characterize therapists who are iatrogenic and probably are dismissed in the training process, or cannot maintain a practice because teachers, colleagues, and patients quickly realize that the rigidity in clinical activity represents serious ego-syntonic characterologic flaws. While most leave the field, unfortunately, some of these therapists gravitate to sinecures in institutions and agencies and may get "kicked upstairs" into administrative posts where they may become the bane of therapists rather than of patients.

Type VI Generalized, conscious, therapist-derived reactions are manifested by therapists who are aware of characterologic problems and who, in spite of therapy, training, and experience cannot come to terms with other rigidities. These therapists tend to move away from close patient contact deliberately, may move out of the field, but if they remain, become excellent researchers, academicians, and administrators.

Type VII Generalized, unconscious patient-induced reactions are found in therapists who are controlled by their patients. While remaining in the field they may be "popular" therapists with their patients, they are likely to be "hypereclectic" in that they are willing to try any type of treatment, and may keep patients in treatment for long periods with little observable personality change. They yield easily to patient demands, tend to gratify rather than analyze, and function in a friendly, informal, "social" atmosphere.

Type VIII Generalized, conscious, patient-induced reactions point to therapists who are well aware of being manipulated by patients, but do not have the emotional ability to challenge, confront, interpret, or otherwise control of the therapeutic interaction. Sometimes young, inexperienced therapists are intimidated by their patients and, out of a fear of losing them (and their fees), yield to the patients' ploys, demands, and resistances. These are usually very insecure and unhappy therapists who either leave the field or who seek psychotherapy or psychoanalysis to resolve the underlying character flaw.

The Communication of Countertransference

Tauber (1954), Little (1951), and child therapists (Colm, 1955; Proctor, 1959; Green, 1972) believe that it is therapeutic to the patient (and therapist?) for the therapist to reveal dreams and feelings. But most authors are circumspect about this issue and generally imply that the countertransference should not be shared with the patient. Gitelson's (1952) statement seems to strike the middle ground: "You can reveal as much of oneself as is needed to foster and support the patient's discovery of the actual interpersonal situation as contrasted with the transference–countertransference situation." Freud's remark, in a 1913 letter to Binswanger (1957), is salient.

> It is one of the most difficult ones technically in psychoanalysis. I regard it as more easily solvable on the theoretical level. What is given to the patient should indeed never be a spontaneous affect, but always consciously allotted, and then more or less of it as the need may arise. Occasionally a great deal, but never from one's unconscious. This I should regard as a formula. In other words, one must always recognize one's counter-transference and rise above it, only then is one free oneself. To give someone too little because one loves him is being unjust to the patient and a technical error. All this is not easy and perhaps possible only if one is older. (p. 50)

Kohrman et al. (1971) suggest that the analyst point out the patient's need to induce particular feelings in the analyst. Rather than "confess" to the induced feelings, the analyst should pursue with the patient the possibility that there are similar hidden and projected feelings within the patient.

My own experience has led me to believe that no gratuitous revelation of countertransference is ever indicated and that countertransference material may be shared only when it will be predictably helpful. When the patient does guess my feeling state, I validate his or her perception in accord with the principle of reinforcing his or her reality testing. One delinquent youngster, who was provocative and destructive in my office asked whether I was mad at him. While affirming his perception, I asked him how that information would be helpful to him. He replied, "It makes me feel good to know what people are really thinking about me and it helps me control myself when I know people are mad at me."

In another situation, an obsessional 7-year-old boy quizzed me incessantly after each of his quasiprovocative moves, "Are you mad at me, doctor?" Interpretations seemed to have no impact on him. Aware of my own growing annoyance, recalling his mother's murderous rage toward him, and mindful of his own internal fury, I quipped half playfully, half seriously, "I'm so mad, I could kill you." Startled, but pleased, he enthused, "You are?" Reaching for some guns, he said, "Now we can play killing each other." At that point we could examine his own disowned murderous feelings, the projection involved, and his wanting to bring others to the point of murdering him without harm coming to him.

CLINICAL STUDIES

Several clinical studies illustrate how Type IV countertransference can be utilized to understand and resolve patient resistances. In effect, a countertransference reflects the presence of and leads to a counterresistance. The counterresistance must be studied, understood, and dissolved by the therapist before being able to resolve the resistances of the patient. The analysis of the counterresistance can frequently lead to an understanding and a derivation of an effective resolution to patient resistance.

In many of the interventions in these cases, classic means of handling resistances are not typically used. The reasons for this have been spelled out in Chapters 2 and 3. Many of the techniques are oriented toward supporting rather than actively analyzing the ego defenses. When the defenses are supported and not attacked, the child or adolescent tends to give them up as resistances and "grow out" of them, especially as the ego experiences less anxiety and develops more adaptive defenses. With children and adolescents whose conflicts are intense or stem largely from preverbal stages of development, joining and mirroring are used to help evolve the narcissistic transference. From this vantage point, the therapist works to resolve the narcissistic transference into an object transference which, in the context of a healthy ego, can be analyzed with more traditional methods.

"Rip Van Winkle"

A 10-year-old boy, Gary, was referred because of limited school performance despite sound potential, poor peer relations

—particularly a tendency to assume the position of scapegoat—and an annoying, teasing manner toward his family. Gary generally tended to project blame onto teachers and peers and did not seem to be involved in exploring himself or his own contributions to his difficulties. The therapy sessions tended to drift unproductively with little emotional contact. The therapist began to dread and be annoyed with the boredom, lack of contact, and unproductivity of the sessions. In particular, the therapist was subject to feelings of fatigue and drowsiness during the sessions, despite his being alert and functioning normally with the patients scheduled before and after Gary. Gary, too, reported feeling sleepy and in fact would close his eyes and nap for short periods. It was apparent that Gary was "acting in" and that the therapist was being induced to "act in" as well. Gary would rationalize his tiredness in terms of a long and arduous school day and unhappy peer experiences. He would persistently quiz the therapist about the need for therapy and nag about its worth. In similar cases when a child or adolescent complains about sleepiness, the resistance usually can be resolved by the therapist's asking, "Why don't you take a nap?" The patient usually will respond by saying that he or she wasn't in therapy to sleep and will go on with the session. Gary, however, took the therapist's question to sanction sleep. As Gary would begin to doze off, the therapist asked, "What should I be doing while you sleep?" In other cases, this would be startling enough to rouse the patient to further communication. However, Gary said he didn't care, the therapist could also take a nap. The therapist then thought he was "up the creek," which he associated to being up the Hudson River, sleeping like Rip Van Winkle. There was also a curious emotional admixture of frustration, annoyance, anger, and not caring about the treatment. The therapist then asked Gary, "How come you'd let me get away with sleeping during your session?" Gary replied casually, "Everybody sleeps a lot in my family." A few more questions revealed that Gary's father, on returning from work, would promptly take a nap. Again, after supper, he would sleep until he went to bed. This depressive pattern of apparently was more or less accepted by Gary as "normal." Gary did admit that he wished his father would play with him instead of sleeping, but had abandoned any hope that the father would change. I told

Gary the story of Rip Van Winkle and asked him if he would like my help in waking up his father. Gary offered an inordinate amount of resistance to this idea, which was not clearly understood. We slowly worked out ways of waking the father and getting more attention from him. Gary's caution became clear about waking the father too abruptly, for he had intuitively understood that the father's depression masked considerable rage. Gary also came to recognize that some of the anger he fantasized in the father was a projection. Gary agreed that the best and most conservative approach would be to demonstrate an interest in the father—that Gary should try to get his father to tell the story of his own life. Gary soon found out that his father, when 7 years old, had lost his own father. Gary then was able to see that his father had lost interest in Gary when he was about 7 years old. As Gary put it, "His father went to sleep on him when he was 7 too." From then on, Gary seemed to "come to life." It appeared that Gary's interest in his father had so deeply touched the father that he in turn (registering the fatherly interest of Gary), became more alive. Gary then was able to recognize his identification with his depressed, uncaring father and to see that his annoying and teasing of others represented the only ways he had known to stay in contact with his father. Further analysis revealed that Gary's withdrawal was based on an earlier abandonment by his mother who left Gary in the care of housekeepers so that she could devote her time to her depressed husband.

Discussion. This case is prototypical of many therapeutic situations where both the patient and therapist are drawn into a therapeutic impasse characterized by mutual "lulling," ennui, and stagnation. The disinterested, uncaring, bored, sleeping, uninvolved patient is easily identified and is well known to us. But the other side of the transference—literally the counterreaction to the transference—is not so easily discerned nor so easily resolved. Who among us likes to stay with and study our own feelings of boredom, lack of care and interest, especially toward a child? Many of these "Rip Van Winkle" children act out the parental feelings to them and induce in the therapist their own feelings of being neglected (Racker's "concordant identification" [1957]) and the parental feelings of neglect ("complementary identification" as introduced by Helene Deutsch, according to Racker [1957, p. 311]).

Many therapists view their induced countertransference feelings as caused by malicious manipulations by the patient. This may be true with patients who are vengeful and want the therapist to suffer as much as they. But the induced countertransference should usually be labeled as a product of an unconscious communication from the patient who recreates those conflictful interpersonal relations or intrapsychic difficulties that he or she has not mastered. In doing so, the patient gives the therapist an opportunity to establish a helpful ambience and/or to intervene in a therapeutic manner. The induction of the countertransference then may be seen as a *cooperative* effort on the part of the patient to engage the therapist, even though lack of contact and distance appears most obvious. This view of the patient's communication is consistent with Searles' (1975) seminal view that the patient is attempting to help, not necessarily hinder, the therapist. Langs' (1975) and Sandler's (1976) emphasis on the patient's attempts to facilitate a helpful therapeutic interrelationship is also relevant.

Ekstein and Caruth (1971) describe a similar case of a 16-year-old schizophrenic boy who induced drowsiness in his therapist. The patient was attempting to assign the therapist to the role of a special kind of echo, to which the therapist unconsciously objected.

The "Ahistoric" Child

Related to the "Rip Van Winkle" child is the "ahistoric" child, who replies with "I don't know," "I don't remember," "I don't care," and otherwise with a "yes" or "no." The presenting symptoms usually involve some behavioral or characterologic disturbance with quasi- or predelinquent behavior, poor school achievement, strained peer relations, and unmanageability at home. The background usually involves neglect and exposure to a series of trauma, particularly violence between the parents leading to a separation. The child seems to live only in the moment, does not wish to recall the past, cannot anticipate, and seemingly does not learn from experience. He or she seems to wear cognitive and emotional blinders, and is without a history. The usual induced countertransference is one of frustration, failure, incompetence, anger, "floating," and impotence. Therapists may feel that none of their training and/or experience has any significance, i.e., that they are professionally ahistoric.

Paul, a 9-year-old, bright-eyed, athletically built youngster, was referred for disruptive behavior in school and home. His mother, who was an interested but somewhat seductive young woman and who obviously enjoyed many of Paul's antics, complained that Paul had not been functioning well in school, was apt to lie, cheat, and steal, was the scourge of the neighborhood, and was uncontrollable at home. She described a stormy marital relationship to a sadistic man who eventually deserted her and their two children. Paul's disruptive behavior appeared coincidentally with the abrupt departure of his father.

In the initial interview, Paul denied any knowledge about the circumstances of his visit with me, indicated that he "sometimes" got into trouble in school, and that he would be willing to let me help him stay out of trouble. When I told him I could best help him if he could tell me the story of his life, his reply was, "I was born and here I am. That's it." Any attempts to get him to elaborate were met by vague, meaningless replies, evasion, and insistence that he had nothing on his mind. He stubbornly claimed that he could not remember anything about his past—even the immediate past of the day. Backing away for several sessions, I allowed him to develop an interest in a racing car set and models. Any of my occasional questions were met with shrugs, "I don't know," and other disclaimers. I noted to him that he liked action and not talk—that he was "a man of action." I also told him that he never appeared to worry and always seemed to have a good time. He agreed enthusiastically.

One day when he entered brightly and cheerfully as always, he asked me what I would like to do. Rather than reply "I'd like to listen to the story of your life," I asked him if he would be willing to help me.

P. (*Surprise, shrug, smile*) I don't know.
T. (*Cheerfully*) That's wonderful.
P. What's wonderful?

T. That you said you didn't know.
P. (*Laughs, looks bewildered*)
T. I really admire the fact that you don't know things.
P. What do you mean?
T. Well, I noticed that you always have a clear mind and that your mind isn't cluttered up with a lot of junk like mine. Also, I admire the fact that you're a carefree guy who really enjoys life although you get into a little trouble once in a while. I have a problem that I think you can help me with. You see, my head is filled with a lot of worries, and I remember a lot of things I want to forget. This is very bad for my health and makes me feel lousy. So what I want you to do is help me to be more like you, that is, not to care about anything or anybody and just forget about everything. (*This was all said in a spirit of an anxious, cheerless, ruminative soul who wanted some relief from his misery.*) How about it?
P. (*Playfully*) I don't know.
T. That's the spirit. Suppose we just go on doing what we've been doing and I'll write down and then practice all the things you say and do so I won't know anything. Can you tell me anything else?
P. Not really.
T. That's a very good one. I'll write it down along with the "I don't know."

For the next several sessions I kept a special sheet of paper ready to record any of his resistive maneuvers. We listed:

I don't care	Huh?
So what?	Eh!
Forget	Could be
So?	Sometimes
Because	It doesn't matter
Who cares?	

As I began to "practice" on him, he was at first pleased while displaying a somewhat tutorial and paternal air. Over the next few sessions, he began to object to my acting like him. At first smilingly, then with some determination, he tried to put a stop to my mirroring him.

P. What should we do today?
T. I don't know.
P. (*Despairingly*) Here we go again.
T. What's wrong with my acting like you?
P. I don't know. Oh, I really hate it when you act like me.
T. Why do you hate it?
P. I just do.
T. That's wonderful—I'll write that down. I really like being like you. I can't understand why you don't like me being like you.

After persistent inquiry into his hatred of his mirrored self and a denied interpretation that he probably hated himself, Paul steadily became more interested in himself and could talk more meaningfully about his life. His behavior during this period, as reported by his school and his mother, improved considerably. When asked whether his behavioral improvement was connected with my acting like him, he demurred and said, "Well, maybe, but I just decided to change my attitude because people didn't like me and I kept getting in trouble."

Discussion. Therapists generally seem to be trained to maintain negative attitudes toward defenses. Defenses and resistances appear to be the despised enemies which need to be analyzed, interpreted, confronted, cracked, and otherwise demolished, particularly when the patient is not overtly cooperative. This adversary and catabolic position appears inappropriate with patients whose ego-defenses are weak and unstable. In essence, this encounter amounts to preanalytic and ego-supportive work. With the "ahistoric" child, we can hypothesize that the negative countertransference feelings are an accurate mirror of those feelings that the child's weak ego cannot endure. Therapists must not only endure these feelings, they should also emphasize the positive aspects of the defense-resistance. After all, by the time the child has reached the therapist, has the child's defensive behavior not been thoroughly criticized, demeaned, and punished at home and school? When the therapist finds a way to value the defense-resistance, a narcissistic transference (mirror transference in Kohut's [1977] terms) is established. That is, the child perceives that he or she and the therapist are the same along certain dimensions. The child can then project and externalize that part of the self he or she hates into the therapist, attack the hated introject, and cease attacking the ego. The child's ego and self-esteem are thus bolstered, especially when the therapist maintains a positive regard for the expelled introject and accompanying defense-resistances. With a strengthened ego, the child becomes less defensive and more reasonable. As the ego matures, the child then is more amenable to traditional psychotherapeutic approaches.

Verbal reflections are useful where the trauma to the ego has occurred *after* the child has reached the point in development where he or she can conceptualize and verbalize the trauma. Many therapists use the cutoff concept of the oedipal stage and talk of preoedipal problems. No particular point in veridical time is relevant. Consideration should be given to the total development of the child: the development of concept formation, verbal expressiveness, and symbolic processes with special emphasis on Piaget's stages. When the trauma has occurred at a preverbal level—when action, thought, and verbalization are still fused—verbal techniques alone are relatively useless. Only emotional communications appear to have any meaningful impact.

"My Heart Belongs to Daddy"

A common situation that induces strong transferences and countertransference reactions occurs with a teenage patient and a therapist of the opposite sex.

A 15-year-old girl who was physically attractive but considerably overweight appeared for her first interview, wearing a large disheveled hat, dirty tattered blue jeans, grimy boots, and wrapped in a well-worn army field jacket. My immediate impression was that she was trying to disguise her innate beauty. She was surly and impudent, suggesting that she wanted to keep herself at considerable emotional distance. She barely alluded to her problems, which consisted of social withdrawal and isolation, depression, and excessive control by her parents.

Although I felt "put off" by her, I also experienced considerable attraction to her along with sensual promptings. Beneath her trappings I could visualize a beautiful and warm young woman. Her inability to trust people, along with my own emotional promptings, immediately raised the unspoken question of whether I could be trusted to use my feelings constructively.

Joyce believed there was something wrong with her since she was unable to trust anyone. My line of questioning, such as "Why do you have to trust anyone?" "What's wrong with being by yourself?" relieved some of the guilt about her mistrust and isolation. She agreed to return largely because she felt I did not "tell" her anything, i.e., made no attempts to control or seduce her.

In the next session she guiltily revealed that she did not trust me. I asked her, "Why in the world should you trust me, a complete stranger?" As Joyce groped to answer the question, she visibly relaxed and began to talk more freely about her circumstances. I was reminded of Heimann's (1950) injunction to sustain and subordinate emotional reactions. During the next few sessions, it became clear to me why I had not been sure I could properly control my own erotic and seductive feelings. Joyce revealed that her father had maintained a paternalistic yet thinly disguised incestuous relationship with an emotionally disturbed sister. Moreover, despite the father's overt disapproval of Joyce's dating and "hanging out" with boys, he would attempt to "debrief" her after every social encounter. In addition, he repeatedly reminded her to think of him while on a date and consistently referred to her as his "best girlfriend." Joyce further intimated that her father saw her as a "young edition" of his wife, whose beauty was now waning.

Joyce began to understand the strong pull of the father and realized that her social isolation was a reflection of her "loyalty" to her father, and that her depression was a result of the internalized rage toward his demands as well as the guilt about her protest and rebelliousness. At one point in this exploration, she exasperatedly exploded with "I guess he wants me to be like the song, 'My Heart Belongs to Daddy.' " My countertransference was parallel to the transference the father was living out with his daughter. An additional source emerged later in treatment after Joyce more comfortably examined her own strong erotic feelings, and still later, her capacity for orgasmic experience. In the first session, she had communicated and induced in me the power of her own hidden sexual feelings.

Discussion. It has been common procedure to match an adolescent with a therapist of the same sex. Various rationales, especially supplying a model for identification, have been used. However, with patients whose difficulties are preverbal, the sex of the therapist makes little difference. In treating regressed patients, the male therapist must come to terms with the fact that he has never had the experience of conceiving, carrying, giving birth to, and suckling a child, and that a Type IV countertransference may be relatively difficult to experience. Nonetheless, patients, if appropriately encouraged, will assist the therapist in developing and maintaining a therapeutic posture.

Anthony (1969) cites the case of a 12-year-old oedipal girl who, insisting on knowing her male therapist's church affiliation, induced discomfort in the therapist. The therapist, recognizing an erotic feeling within himself, interpretated the inquiry as a form of flirtation and commended the girl for growth in feminine development.

Jones and Gehman (1971) explore the emotional impact of adolescent girls' virginity on their male therapists.

The Elective Mute

Greg, a 7-year-old, came to treatment because of his elective mutism with strangers and in school. Greg's parents, who were not very articulate and quite defensive, provided a limited developmental history and no clues to his mutism. Their silences and lack of spontaneity, especially with the father present, induced feelings of frustration, annoyance, and lack of direction in the therapist.

When Greg came to the initial interview he appeared somber, with searching eyes, and he would occasionally flash a quick, unreal smile. Since I realized that he would not talk to me, I told him it was not necessary to talk, but we would find some way of understanding each other, perhaps with our faces, particularly our eyes and mouth. He nodded in agreement and began to play with toys. There was no discernible pattern in his play except that he enjoyed crashing cars together. The ensuing weeks brought no change in the sessions, and no change in his behavior outside of the sessions. I experienced mounting frustration and helplessness. Occasionally he would motion to me to join him in his play. Quite surprisingly, I found myself irritated with him and set limits prematurely and too firmly. Moreover, when he became absorbed in his play and ignored me, I experienced a sense of relief and drowsiness. I started condemning myself as being a poor therapist—uninterested and dull. I wondered why I ever accepted the case and how I could get rid of him. At about this time, Greg's mother happened to mention that Greg's father liked to watch sports on TV and alluded to the fact that he would tolerate no interference with his pastime. She also intimated that he would go to sleep early, but quickly, and protectively added that he worked very hard during the day.

When Greg began to giggle or cry out in his play, I then ordered him not to make any sounds. At first he was taken aback, then smiled and giggled more openly. As I escalated my demands for quiet, he, just as deliberately and pleasurably, defied me and made various sounds with his mouth and toys. I fantasized myself as the father who wanted peace and quiet and thus began to experiment with various ways of quieting Greg. I sought to recreate the climate in which Greg's mutism evolved. The basic formula that brought squeals of delight from him was "Shut up or I'll kill you!" After we repeated this several times I interpreted the parallel between our scene and what occurred with his father. We improvised and elaborated on the theme. For example, as I would make a gesture to grab him, he would pull out a gun and shoot me. Greg would fall off his feet in laughter as I feigned a convulsive death. He agreed to have the parents come in to view our game. They found remarkable similarities to what went on at home and agreed to some guidance in this area. The school at this time reported a "miraculous" change in Greg who not only began to talk, but was on his way to becoming a popular leader in his class.

The Daredevil

Joe was a 15-year-old who completely fit the diagnosis "unsocialized aggressive reaction of adolescence." He had terrorized, angered, and alienated all with whom he had contact. He had often angered me with his behavior in my office. Besides his aggressiveness toward others, Joe frequently would engage in near self-destructive acts particularly with his trail motorcycle. He was certain that he would not live until the age of 20. After one particularly hair-raising accident where he suffered considerable cuts and bruises, he was bragging in a counterphobic manner about how much fun he had had and went on to talk about further dangerous stunts similar to professional daredevils.

T. Do you want to kill yourself?
J. I don't care.
T. How about my killing you?
J. How?
T. Anyway you'd like. How about my throwing you off a cliff?
J. Nothing doing.
T. Why not?
J. I don't want to die.

A few weeks later when Joe began to revive his self-destructive tendencies on his motorbike:

T. Do you have any insurance?
J. What's that?
T. *(Explains the concept of life insurance, premium payments, and beneficiaries.)*
J. So what?
T. Well, suppose I take out a million dollar policy on your life and when you kill yourself, I'll collect a million bucks.
J. You dirty rotten son of a bitch. I wouldn't give you the satisfaction.
T. What do you mean?
J. I wouldn't kill myself for you.

T. You're going to kill yourself anyway—so why not?
J. Well I'm not going to kill myself period. Go fuck yourself!

Later in the session, Joe reverted to glorifying his death-defying stunts.

T. How about my advertising your new stunt for next weekend and I'll charge admission—say 5 bucks a head. People will pay anything to see someone risk their life and maybe get hurt. Maybe 10. You do your thing and I'll make some money on it.
J. You crazy son of a bitch. You're crazier than I am. I'm not going to do anything like that.
T. Why not?
J. It's too crazy.
T. You don't care if you hurt yourself or not and besides people pay lots of money to see other people get hurt.
J. Forget about it! Let's talk about something else.

Discussion. This intervention effectively quelled Joe's self-destructive acts on his motorcycle and led to his despairing confession of his father's "craziness," drinking, threats, neglect, and abuse of him and his mother. Although radical, this intervention was consciously and deliberately made with the following intent: (a) to establish a narcissistic transference relative to his murderous, "crazy" impulses; (b) to obtain control of his harsh superego; and (c) to allow a projection onto me of his "craziness" and destructive impulses so that his ego could see more clearly what he was doing to himself. Interventions of this sort should only be made when the therapist fully understands and controls the therapeutic situation and the etiology of his or her countertransference. In Joe's situation, my countertransference approach derived from the feelings of the sadistic mother and father who wished their son to be incapacitated. I appeared to Joe as reflecting a basic attitude of the parents and his own internalized destructive feelings. His ability to object to these representations was seen as a positive therapeutic step that probably occurred because I established a narcissistic transference. When he felt secure in the narcissistic transference, he could then use me as a helpful object. Tylum (1978) explains this process in terms of patients seeing their missing parts in the analyst.

In the treatment of delinquents, the establishment of a narcissistic transference may provide the foundation for a successful therapeutic relationship because they more easily tolerate a narcissistic relationship and cannot sustain an object relationship. When delinquents perceive that the therapist is like themselves, the narcissistic transference is established. They are at ease in this relationship because it recreates the relatively comfortable relationship with the mother preceding the traumatic separation–individuation phase. Within the security of the narcissistic–symbiotic relationship, they begin to experience the terrifying feelings that originally occurred when their symbiosis was broken and when they were not supported in this separation–individuation stage.

Furor Therapeuticus

An obsessive–compulsive child was being treated for his "thoughts" by a therapist-in-training. Because the therapy seemed to be hopelessly bogged down, the supervisor interviewed the child and asked him why the treatment was not going well. The child responded in effect, "Mr. T. has too many thoughts himself to really help me. Instead of paying attention to me, he just sits there and pays attention to his thoughts of curing me of my thoughts." When the child was asked how his therapist could really help him the boy said, "He should just listen and try to understand me." When the therapist-in-training was relieved of his *"furor therapeuticus,"* progress resumed.

A Mothering Man

Joan, a 17-year-old, had been suicidally depressed. She had induced profound feelings of hopelessness, helplessness, and near immobilization in her therapist. With Joan in a catatoniclike trance, her therapist asked how he could help her. She replied by commenting on a ray of light shining on the therapist's forehead. On inquiry, Joan determined that the light represented a ray of hope that the therapist could become a "mothering man"—her only possibility of survival. Joan wrote

> Blue clouds given boundaries by white skies
> softened with light green leaves
> billowing in the spinnaker of birth
> sail over rough seas
> to reach its destiny.
>
> Gray masses come thundering down
> dampening all life
> to be given;
> forcing it away from
> the bearer of individual lives.
>
> A ray of light struggles
> through blue clouds
> concealing itself
> within the mind of
> one mothering man
> who painfully reveals
> one dormant life
> that was forced.

Over a long period of time Joan instructed the therapist about how the transformation could occur. Supervision by a woman was also helpful in engendering the therapist's capacity to provide the emotional contact and care Joan needed to grow. The induced feelings of helplessness and immobilization were her way of emotionally communicating how she felt when in a trance and with her mother. The induced feelings were probably similar to the emotional position of Joan's mother, who was unable to nurture her baby. Later, Joan documented her mother's disregard for her while an infant and her father's inept but dutiful attention to her rearing.

Nine years after termination, the therapist wrote to Joan requesting permission to cite her poem and the clinical circumstances. Joan offered the following:

> I guess you were the ray of light warming life and the world (my world) around me. The world and life that I was refusing and turning away, forcing away. You were making me face up to life as much as I was turning away. You tried many times to pull me back to life when I was in one of my trances and unwilling to come alive. You kept pulling in our tug of war to have me come into the world you labored hard and long. I gather I was no easy delivery—to get me to see that life is worth living if we only give each other a chance.

The Parental Complexity

The literature describing treatment approaches to parents is enormous. It spins off into various modalities such as group therapy, family therapy, and child guidance, and cuts across the psychotherapeutic disciplines. However, a review of the literature reveals that there is no clear-cut concept of countertransference toward parental figures. Nor is there any significant body of knowledge organized around the concept. Again, we ask, "Why so little?" And again a suggested answer: "Because there's so much." We are also reminded of Freud's declinations in dealing with parents.

The complexity of the countertransference situation is increased as the number of therapeutic adjunctive relationships is increased. The scope of the area is so large that it cannot be adequately covered in this chapter. Therefore, only one type of case will be presented: that of the symbiotic child and mother. This situation is common, not fully explored in the literature, and fraught with grave countertransference pitfalls. In keeping with my general thesis—that Type IV countertransference can enhance the therapy—some background material will be presented to delineate the seeming countertransference obstacles and also to suggest how to turn them into useful instruments.

The first issue is one of diagnosis. The initial telephone contact not only provides important diagnostic clues, but may influence the mother's decision to accept the exploration of therapy. Quite typically, the mother indicates that her husband cannot or will not come in. Moreover, she gives the impression that she expects to be seen with her child. The fusion is apparent in the mother's absorption in the child or adolescent. Allusions to altered body boundaries such as "He gets under my skin" or "My heart beats for her" supply important clues. The amount of time that mother and child spend together, the presence of a school phobia, or the mother's preoccupation with the child to the extent of the neglect of her own needs are other signs. There frequently is a negative cast to the relationship in which mother and child criticize, belittle, or otherwise claw at each other. One gets the feeling that they cannot let each other alone, that they cannot live with each other, and yet cannot live without each other. This close binding relationship does not only occur between mother and child. A father who spends considerable time at home may engage in typical symbiotic relationships.

The common response to the symbiotic dyad by schools (Sperling, 1961), institutions, and even some therapists is "break it up," as if the symbiosis poses some threat to the observer. Some clinics correctly insist that the mother be in treatment. However, by insisting that mother and child have different therapists, the case may founder. The inclination to "break it up" may be an important diagnostic and countertransference clue.

One important indication of the degree of symbiosis is the force with which the mother controls the child, and ultimately seeks to control the therapy. In the initial stages, this control can seldom be successfully challenged without deleterious effect. Moreover, the control may be only subtly manifested as with the mother who develops a severe but medically puzzling gastroenteritis when her school phobic son begins to attend school again. Her need to control can be seen as a crucial, if not last ditch, defense of hers and should be temporarily maintained and responded to with the utmost respect. The initial countertransference reaction of the therapist is apt to be an indignant "No," or "Who do you think you are telling me how to treat your child?" These responses hark back to the therapist's own individuation–separation phase and, if not understood and handled constructively, will result in therapeutic chaos. The experience of being controlled by the parent, and the natural rising negativistic tendencies of the therapist can have two implications. One is the reverberation of the healthy impulse of the child resisting the mother's untoward influence. Spitz (1957) offers an excellent account of the developmental meaning of the child's "No." The second is that the force of the resistance is a clue to the intensity of the mother's need for fusion. Her need to control reflects her defensive vulnerability. Frequently the mother will reveal much later that she had been terrified of losing her child and of losing control of herself. Sometimes, with her demands and volatility, she can induce in the therapist the anxiety and terror against which she is trying to protect herself.

Where the child seems to be successfully opposing the symbiotic needs of the mother, it may be assumed that the mother is anxious about losing her symbiotic object, and will be looking for someone with whom she can reestablish her symbiotic equilibrium. The therapist should be available to establish that relationship with her. One way that usually relieves the mother's anxiety, and still allows a working relationship, is asking the mother for *her* opinion and guidance. As soon as she senses that the therapist will not upset the balance, will not spirit away her child, and not cast her adrift, she becomes more cooperative. When she senses that the therapist is flexible and respects the symbiosis, she becomes more cooperative. The aim in the treatment of the symbiotic mother–child dyad is to provide therapy not only for the child but for the mother and consequently for the relationship. This is achieved by the therapist becoming the symbiotic object for mother and child, respectively, and then resolving that relationship into an object relationship. Sometimes, in the initial interview, the mother will consider individual treatment for herself. Often, it takes years before she will accept such help for herself. Still, when she will not accept therapy nor guidance, she may be willing to accept the role of "co-therapist," and "take lessons" from the child's therapist. The development of "filial therapy" by Guerney (1964), S. Marshall (1978), and others is of interest in this regard. Freud (1909) established this therapeutic paradigm in the treatment of Little Hans.

As the mother (and child) become more involved in the therapeutic situation, the role of the father slowly emerges. At first he seems conspicuous by the neglect attributed to him. As mother and child weave the father into the sessions, he tends to be vague, shadowy, and ambivalent. He then takes on a more negative valence, evoking in the therapist questions such as, "How can he be so neglectful or unfeeling or brutal." If the father has not been a part of the therapeutic scene, he should be involved, for three reasons. First, the therapist can really test his or her own countertransference attitudes. Frequently the father is not what he is represented to be. Secondly, the father may need help in becoming the affective object of the mother. Thirdly, without the father's involvement, the negative countertransference reactions of the therapist may be amplified and played back by the mother and child to the father so that he is pushed out of the therapeutic field completely. Grunebaum and Strean (1964) review the neglect of fathers in child guidance. Rubenstein and Levitt (1957) formulate some excellent hypotheses regarding the therapist's identification with the patient and the subsequent countertransference reactions to the patient's father.

In the following case, the pathology of the family was blatant and seemingly begging for treatment. The parents recognized considerable marital maladjustment but closed this area off essentially saying, "If you try to investigate our marriage we will take our child out of treatment." They explained that they had had marital counseling and that a satisfactory *modus operandi* had been worked out. They implied that both were affectively cold and could live more or less emotionally separate lives together. According to Mrs. R., the daughter, Ruth, seemed to be a clinging, whining, dependent 8-year-old. Ruth certainly was deeply invested in her mother, largely as a function of a separation from her ill mother when Ruth was 8 months old. However, she was more deeply involved with peers and school than her mother perceived. Mrs. R., while seeming to be a haughty and detached person who could not abide Ruth's needs for closeness, actually derived considerable emotional satisfaction from her relationship with Ruth.

Accepting the warning from the parents, the therapist agreed to see Ruth once a week, the mother once a month, and the father as needed. The therapist felt that to separate mother and daughter by providing each with a different therapist would have created havoc. The therapist slowly accelerated Mrs. R.'s schedule to once a week which she grudgingly accepted. The aim was simple. The therapist tried to become Mrs. R.'s symbiotic object, thus displacing Ruth. At the same time, the therapist insinuated himself into Ruth's psychologic structure as her symbiotic object.

The therapist's countertransference to the mother was one of feeling burdened and emotionally cold and distant. The therapist dreaded the sessions for there were long stony, uncomfortable silences, as well as biting skepticism and criticism of the therapist. What was the meaning of the transference–countertransference? Mrs. R. was relating to the therapist as her own mother had related to her, with cold silences and neglect punctuated by sharp rejecting reproaches. The unconscious message was "I wish I could get rid of you, but I can't." Mrs. R. was also treating the therapist as she related to her daughter. To complete the cycle, the therapist reverberated with a similar countertransference feeling: wanting to get rid of the mother.

In the midst of Mrs. R.'s complaints about Ruth's trying behavior, the therapist asked if it was feasible to get rid of Ruth. Mrs. R. dropped her severe mien and burst into an uncontrollable giggle. When she recovered, she attacked the therapist for his hardheartedness, then admitted she had thought about the idea, but had resigned herself to keeping her daughter. As Mrs. R. worked through her guilt, she also revealed that she felt that she had been a terrible mother. When the therapist joined her denigrating defense by telling her that he had known about her deficiencies for a long time, Mrs. R. sighed with relief about not having to keep up her pretenses with the therapist. In this more easy emotional flow, the therapist began to search for other ways to lessen the sessions' dullness and heaviness. Mrs. R. was able to talk about her education and training as a statistician and then began to tell the story of her own life. As the therapist was able to shake free of his rejecting attitude and to see Mrs. R. in a more positive and accepting light, a parallel occurred in the mother–daughter relationship. It appeared that Mrs. R. had identified herself with the positive regard of the therapist which provided her with a role model in her reactions to Ruth.

From time to time the father was requested to come in with his wife to make sure that he was supporting the therapy and to determine whether any inroad could be made into the marital impasse.

Ruth's therapy was ended when she showed consistent signs of operating as a relatively autonomous person, i.e., enjoying sleep-away camp, maintaining good peer relations, yet enjoying a cooperative role in her family. Mrs. R. remained in therapy, overtly to help Ruth consolidate her gains, but covertly to continue her own emotional growth. Mrs. R. terminated her own therapy when she had established herself vocationally. In effect, her symbiotic tie with Ruth was transferred to the therapist, worked through, and its residues displaced into her work.

Concluding Statement

The lack of attention to countertransference in the treatment of children and adolescents appears to be due to several factors. The primary variable appears to be the variety and strength of affects evoked in the therapist which in turn produce anxiety, guilt, and a range of defensive reactions. Defenses against hostile and sexual feelings appear to be central.

Countertransference reactions have traditionally been treated as anathema. However, in the past 25 years a few child therapists, generally more cautious than adult therapists, have begun to explore the potential value of countertransference clues.

Eight types of countertransference reactions are derived around the axes of three variables: (a) the source of the countertransference, i.e., patient-induced or therapist-derived; (b) the extent of awareness of the countertransference by the therapist, i.e., conscious or unconscious; and (c) the degree of specificity or generality of countertransferences.

Type I, wherein therapists are dominated by their own unconscious reactions, is the most therapeutically pernicious while Type IV, wherein the therapist is aware of feelings induced by the patient, holds the most potential for therapeutic understanding and constructive intervention. Types V–VIII represent reactions that rest on characterologic flaws that should disqualify the therapist from practice.

REFERENCES

Abbate, G. M. Panel: Child analysis at different developmental stages. *Journal American Psychoanalytic Association,* 1964, *12,* 136–150.

Ackerman, N. W. Transference and countertransference. *Psychoanalytic Review,* 1956, *46,* 17–28.

Adams, J. W. *Psychoanalysis of drug dependence: The understanding and treatment of a particular form of pathological narcissism,* New York: Grune & Stratton, 1978.

Adler, A. Cited in Ansbacher, H. L. and Ansbacher, R. R. *The individual psychology of Alfred Adler.* New York: Basic Books, 1956.

Aichhorn, A. *Wayward youth.* New York: Viking Press, 1935.

Aichhorn, A. *Delinquency and child guidance: Selected papers* (O. Fleischmann, P. Kramer, & H. Ross, Eds.). New York: International Universities Press, 1964.

Akeret, R. U., & Stockhamer, N. Countertransference reactions to college drop-outs. *American Journal of Psychotherapy,* 1955, *19,* 622–632.

Anthony, E. J. The reactions of adults to adolescents and their behavior. In G. Caplan & S. Lebovici (Eds.), *Psychosocial perspectives.* New York: Basic Books, 1969.

Anthony, E. J. Nonverbal and verbal systems of communication. *Psychoanalytic Study of the Child,* 1977, *32,* 307–325.

Appelbaum, S. A. *Out in inner space: A psychoanalyst explores the new therapies.* Garden City, New York: Anchor Press/Doubleday, 1979.

Ayllon, T. Intensive treatment of psychiatric behavior by stimulus satiation and food reinforcement. *Behavior Research Therapy,* 1963, *1,* 53–61.

Bandler, R., & Grinder, J. *Patterns of the hypnotic techniques of Milton H. Erickson, M.D.* (Vol. I). Cupertino, California: Meta Publications, 1975.

Bandura, A., Lipsher, D. H., and Miller, P. E. Psychotherapists' approach-avoidance reactions to patients' expression of hostility. *Journal of Consulting Psychology,* 1960, 24, 1–8.

Bandura, A. Psychotherapists' anxiety level, self insight and psychotherapeutic competence. *Journal of Abnormal and Social Psychology,* 1956, 52, 333–337.

Baranger, M., & Baranger, W. Insight—the analytic situation. In R. E. Litman (Ed.), *Psychoanalysis in the Americas.* New York: International Universities Press, 1966.

Bell, J. E. *Family therapy.* New York: Jason Aronson, 1975.

Berg, B., & Rosenblum, N. Fathers in family therapy: A survey of family therapists. *Journal of Marriage and Family Counseling,* 1977, *3,* 85–91.

Berlin, I. N. *Bibliography for training in child psychiatry.* New York: Human Sciences Press, 1976.

Bernstein, I., & Glenn, J. The child analyst's emotional reactions to his patients. In J. Glenn (Ed.), *Child Analysis and Therapy.* New York: Jason Aronson, 1978.

Bettleheim, B. The love that is enough: Countertransference and the ego processes of staff members in a therapeutic milieu. In P. Giovacchini (Ed.), *Tactics and techniques in psychoanalytic theory* (Vol. 2). New York: Basic Books, 1975.

Bick, E. Symposium on child analysis: I. Child analysis today. *International Journal of PsychoAnalysis,* 1962, *43,* 328–332.

Binswanger, L. *Sigmund Freud: Reminiscences of a friendship.* New York: Grune and Stratton, 1957.

Blos, P. Berta Bornstein, 1899–1971. *Psychoanalytic study of the child,* 1974, *29,* 35–40.

Bornstein, B. Emotional barriers in the understanding and treatment of children. *American Journal of Orthopsychiatry,* 1948, *18,* 691–697.

Bornstein, B. On latency. *Psychoanalytic Study of the Child,* 1951, *6,* 279–285.

Bornstein, B. The writings of Berta Bornstein. *Psychoanalytic Study of the Child,* 1974, *29,* 29–40.

Brody, S. Some aspects of transference resistance in puberty. *Psychoanalytic Study of the Child,* 1961, *16,* 251–274.

Brandt, L. W. Experiments in psychoanalysis. *Psychoanalytic Review,* 1974, *61,* 95–98.

Bricker, D. O., & Bricker, W. A. *A language intervention program for developmentally young children.* MCCD Monograph Series, No. 1. Miami: University of Miami, 1976.

Burlingham, D. Simultaneous analysis of mother and child. *Psychoanalytic Study of the Child,* 1955, *10,* 165–186.

Burlingham, D. *Psychoanalytic studies of the sighted and the blind.* New York: International Universities Press, 1972.

Carter, E. A., & Orfanidis, M. M. Family therapy with one person and the family therapist's own family in family therapy. In P. J. Guerin (Ed.), *Theory and practice.* New York: Gardner Press, 1976.

Casuso, G. Panel: The relationship between child analysis and the theory and practice of adult psychoanalysis. *Journal of the American Psychoanalytic Association,* 1965, *13,* 159–171.

Chessick, R. D. *Why psychotherapists fail.* New York: Science House, 1971.

Christ, A. E. Sexual countertransference problems with a psychotic child. *Journal of Child Psychiatry,* 1964, *3,* 329–352.

Cohen, M. B. Countertransference and anxiety. *Psychiatry,* 1952, *15,* 231–243.

Cohler, B. J. The significance of the therapist's feelings in the treatment of anorexia nervosa. In S. C. Feinstein & P. Giovacchini (Eds.), *Adolescent psychiatry* (Vol. V). New York: Jason Aronson, 1977.

Colm, H. A field theory approach to transference and its particular application to children. *Psychiatry,* 1955, *18,* 329–352.

Corday, R. J. Limitations of therapy in adolescence. *Journal of Child Psychiatry,* 1967, *6,* 526–538.

Crisp, A. H. "Transference," "symptom emergence" and "social repercussion" in behavior therapy. *British Journal of Medical Psychology,* 1966, *39,* 179–196.

D'Alessio, G. The concurrent use of behavior modification and psychotherapy. *Psychotherapy: Theory, Research and Practice*, 1968, *5,* 175–179.

Daniels, M. *Resistance in psychoanalytic psychotherapy.* G. D. Goldman and D. S. Millman (Eds.). Reading, Mass.: Addison-Wesley, 1980.

Daniels, R. S. Some early manifestations of transference: Their implications for the first phase of psychoanalysis. *Journal of the American Psychoanalytic Association,* 1969, *17,* 995–1014.

Darwin, C. A biographical sketch of an infant. *Mind,* 1877, *2,* 285–294.

De Mause, L. The evolution of childhood. *History of Childhood Quarterly,* 1974, *1,* 503–575. (a)

De Mause, L. (Ed.). *The History of Childhood.* New York: Psychohistory Press, 1974. (b)

Des Lauriers, A. M. & Carlson, C. F. *Your child is asleep: Early infantile autism.* Homewood, Ill: Dorsey Press, 1969.

Dorfman, E. Play therapy. In C. R. Rogers (Ed.), *Client-centered therapy.* Boston: Houghton-Mifflin, 1951.

Dunlap, K. A revision of the fundamental law of habit formation. *Science,* 1928, *67,* 360–362.

Durkin, R. Social functions of psychological interpretations. *American Journal of Orthopsychiatry,* 1967, *37,* 956–962.

Eisnitz, A. Mirror dreams. *Journal of the American Psychoanalytic Association,* 1961, *9,* 461–479.

Ekstein, R. *Children of time and space, of action and impulse.* New York: Appleton-Century-Crofts, 1966.

Ekstein, R. The process of termination and its relation to outcome in the treatment of psychotic disorders in adolescents. In S. C. Feinstein & P. L. Giovacchini (Eds.), *Adolescent psychiatry* (Vol. VI). Chicago: University of Chicago Press, 1978.

Ekstein, R., & Caruth, E. Certain phenomenological aspects of the countertransference in the treatment of schizophrenic children. In R. Ekstein (Ed.), *The challenge: Despair and hope in the conquest of inner space.* New York: Brunner/Mazel, 1971.

Ekstein, R., & Friedman, S. On some current models in the psychoanalytic treatment of childhood psychosis. In R. Ekstein (Ed.), *The challenge: Despair and hope in the conquest of inner space.* New York: Brunner/Mazel, 1971.

Ekstein, R., Wallerstein, J., & Mandelbaum, A. Countertransference in the residential treatment of children: Treatment failure in a child with a symbiotic psychosis. *Psychoanalytic Study of the Child,* 1959, *14,* 186–218. New York: International Universities Press.

Elkisch, P. The psychological significance of the mirror. *Journal of the American Psychoanalytic Association,* 1957, *5,* 235–244.

Epstein, L. The therapeutic function of hate in the countertransference.

Contemporary Psychoanalysis, 1977, *13,* 442–461. Reprinted in L. Epstein and A. H. Feiner (Eds.), *Countertransferences,* New York: Aronson, 1979.

Epstein L., & Feiner, A. H. (Eds). *Countertransference.* New York: Aronson, 1979.

Erickson, M. H. (1952) Deep hypnosis and its induction in *Advanced techniques of hypnosis and therapy: Selected papers of Milton H. Erickson, M.D.* J. Haley (Ed.). New York: Grune & Stratton, 1967.

Erickson, M. H. (1964) An hypnotic technique for resistant patients: the patient, the technique and its rationale and field experiments. In *Advanced techniques of hypnosis and therapy: Selected papers of Milton H. Erickson, M.D.* J. Haley (Ed.). New York: Grune & Stratton, 1967.

Erickson, M. H. (1965) The use of symptoms as an integral part of hypnotherapy. In *Advanced techniques of hypnosis and therapy: Selected papers of Milton H. Erickson, M.D.* J. Haley (Ed.). New York: Grune & Stratton, 1967.

Erikson, K. T. Notes on the sociology of deviance. In Becker, H. (Ed.), *The other side.* New York: Free Press, 1964.

Feather, B. W., & Rhoads, J. M. Psychodynamic behavior therapy: II. Clinical aspects. *Archives of General Psychiatry,* 1972, *26,* 503–511. (a)

Feather, B. W., & Rhoads, J. M. Psychodynamic behavior therapy: Theory and rationale. *Archives of General Psychiatry,* 1972, *26,* 496–502. (b)

Federn, P. *Ego psychology and the psychosis.* New York: Basic Books, 1952.

Feiner, A. H. Lowering the barriers to psychoanalysis. *Contemporary Psychoanalysis,* 1977, *13,* 116–125.

Feldman, Y. The early history of modern psychoanalysis. *Modern Psychoanalysis,* 1978, *3,* 15–28.

Fenichel, O. *Concerning the theory of psychoanalytic technique.* First Series. New York: W. W. Norton 1953[1935].

Fenichel, O. *Problems of psychoanalytic technique.* New York: Psychoanalytic Quarterly, 1941.

Fergelson, C. The mirror dream. *Psychoanalytic Study of the Child,* 1975, *30,* 341–355.

Fergelson, C. On the essential characteristics of child analysis. *Psychoanalytic Study of the Child,* 1977, *32,* 353–361.

Fossey, D. Making friends with mountain gorillas. *National Geographic,* 1970, *137,* 48–67.

Fossey, D. More years with mountain gorillas. *National Geographic,* 1971, *140,* 574–585.

Fouts, G. T. Imitation in children: the effect of being imitated. JSAS *Catalog of Selected Documents in Psychology* 1972, 2, 105.

Fouts, G. T. Effects of being imitated and awareness in the behavior of introverted and extroverted youth *Child Development,* 1975, 46, 296–300.

Fraiberg, S. Some considerations in the introduction to therapy in puberty. *Psychoanalytic Study of the Child,* 1955, *10,* 264–286.

Framo, J. L. Rationale and techniques of intensive family therapy. In I. Boszormenyi-Nagy & J. L. Framo (Eds.), *Intensive family therapy: Theoretical and practical aspects.* New York: Harper & Row, 1965.

Frankl, V. E. *Man's search for meaning: An introduction to logotherapy.* Boston: Beacon Press, 1959.

Frankl, V. E. Paradoxical intention. *American Journal of Psychotherapy,* 1960, *14,* 520–535.

Freud, A. (1926[1927]). Preparation for child analysis. *The writings of Anna Freud* (Vol. I) 3–18. New York: International Universities Press, 1974. (a)

Freud, A. (1926[1927]). The role of transference in the analysis of children. *The writings of Anna Freud* (Vol. I), 36–49. New York: International Universities Press, 1974. (b)

Freud, A. (1936). The ego and the mechanisms of defense. *The writings of Anna Freud* (Vol. II). New York: International Universities Press, 1966.

Freud, A. (1960). Introduction to Kata Levy's "Simultaneous analysis of a mother and her adolescent daughter." *The writings of Anna Freud* (Vol. V), 479–482. New York: International Universities Press, 1960.

Freud, A. (1965). Normality and pathology in childhood: Assessment of development. *The writings of Anna Freud* (Vol. VI). New York: International Universities Press, 1965.

Freud, A. (1970[1957]). Problems of termination in child analysis. *The writings of Anna Freud* (Vol. VII), 3–21. New York: International Universities Press, 1971.

Freud, S. (1893–1895). Studies in hysteria. *The standard edition of the complete psychological works of Sigmund Freud* (Vol. 2). London: Hogarth Press, 1964.

Freud, S. (1905[1904]). On psychotherapy. *The standard edition of the complete psychological works of Sigmund Freud* (Vol. 7), 255–268. London: Hogarth Press, 1964.

Freud, S. (1905). Three essays on the theory of sexuality. *The standard edition of the complete psychological works of Sigmund Freud* (Vol. 7), 125–245. London: Hogarth Press, 1964.

Freud, S. (1909). Analysis of a phobia in a five-year-old boy. *The standard edition of the complete psychological works of Sigmund Freud* (Vol. 10), 1–147. London: Hogarth Press, 1964.

Freud, S. (1910[1909]). Five lectures on psycho-analysis. *The standard edition of the complete psychological works of Sigmund Freud* (Vol. 11), 1–55. London: Hogarth Press, 1964.

Freud, S. (1910). The future prospects of psycho-analytic therapy. *The standard edition of the complete psychological works of Sigmund Freud* (Vol. 11), 139–151. London: Hogarth Press, 1964. (a)

Freud, S. (1910). "Wild" psychoanalysis. *The standard edition of the complete psychological works of Sigmund Freud* (Vol. 11), 219–227. London: Hogarth Press, 1964. (b)

Freud, S. (1913). The disposition to obsessional neurosis. *The standard edition of the complete psychological works of Sigmund Freud* (Vol. 12), 311–325. London: Hogarth Press, 1964.

Freud, S. (1914). On the history of the psychoanalytic movement. *The standard edition of the complete psychological works of Sigmund Freud* (Vol. 14), 7–66. London: Hogarth Press, 1964.

Freud, S. (1917[1916–17]). Introductory lectures on psychoanalysis. *The standard edition of the complete psychological works of Sigmund Freud* (Vol. 16). London: Hogarth Press, 1964.

Freud, S. (1923[1922]). Remarks on the theory and practice of dream-interpretation. *The standard edition of the complete psychological works of Sigmund Freud* (Vol. 19), 102–121. London: Hogarth Press, 1964.

Freud, S. (1925). Negation. *The standard edition of the complete psychological works of Sigmund Freud* (Vol. 19), 235–239. London: Hogarth Press, 1964. (a)

Freud, S. (1925). Preface to Aichhorn's *Wayward youth. The standard edition of the complete psychological works of Sigmund Freud* (Vol. 19), 273–275. London: Hogarth Press, 1964. (b)

Freud, S. (1926). The question of lay analysis. *The standard edition of the complete psychological works of Sigmund Freud* (Vol. 20), 177–249. London: Hogarth Press, 1964.

Freud, S. (1933[1932]). New introductory lectures on psychoanalysis. *The standard edition of the complete psychological works of Sigmund Freud* (Vol. 22), 3–182. London: Hogarth Press, 1964.

Freud, S. (1937). Analysis terminable and interminable. *The standard edition of the complete psychological works of Sigmund Freud* (Vol. 23), 209–253. London: Hogarth Press, 1964.

Freud, S. (1940[1938]). An outline of psycho-analysis. *The standard edition of the complete psychological works of Sigmund Freud* (Vol. 23), 141–207. London: Hogarth Press, 1964. (a)

Freud, S. (1940[1938]). Splitting of the ego in the process of defense. *The standard edition of the complete psychological works of Sigmund Freud* (Vol. 23), 271–278. London: Hogarth Press, 1964. (b)

Friend, M. R. Psychoanalysis of adolescents. In B. B. Wolman (Ed.), *Handbook of child psychoanalysis.* New York: Van Nostrand Reinhold Co., 1972.

Gallup, G. G., Jr. Self recognition in primates: A comparative approach to the bidirectional properties of consciousness. *American Psychologist,* 1977, 32, 329–338.

Gardner, R. A. Helping children cooperate in therapy. In J. Noshpitz (Ed.), *Basic handbook of child psychiatry* (Vol. III). New York: Basic Books, 1979.

Gardner, R. A. *Psychotherapeutic approaches to the resistant child.* New York: Aronson, 1975.

Gardner, G. E. (Ed.) Case studies in childhood emotional disabilities (Vol. 2) New York: American Orthopsychiatric Association, 1956.

Gardner, G. E. (Ed.) Case studies in childhood emotional disabilities (Vol. 1) New York: American Orthopsychiatric Association, 1953.

Giovacchini, P. L. The difficult adolescent patient: Countertransference problems. In S. C. Feinstein & P. L. Giovacchini (Eds.), *Adolescent psychiatry* (Vol. III). New York: Basic Books, 1974.

Giovacchini, P. L. Productive procrastination: Technical factors in the treatment of the adolescent. In S. C. Feinstein & P. L. Giovacchini (Eds.), *Adolescent psychiatry* (Vol. IV). New York: Basic Books, 1975.

Gitelson, M. The emotional position of the analyst in the psycho-analytic situation. *International Journal of PsychoAnalysis,* 1952, *33,* 1–11.

Glover, E. *The techniques of psychoanalysis.* New York: International Universities Press, 1955.

Green, M. R. The interpersonal approach to child therapy. In B. B.

Wolman (Ed.), *Handbook of child psychoanalysis.* New York: Van Nostrand Reinhold Co., 1972.

Greenacre, P. Problems of overidealization of the analyst and of analysis: Their manifestations in the transference and countertransference relationship *Psychoanalytic Study of the Child* 1966, 21, 193–212.

Greenson, R. *The technique and practice of psychoanalysis.* New York: International Universities Press, 1967.

Grinstein, A. *The index of psychoanalytic writings.* New York: International Universities Press, 1974.

Grunebaum, H. E., & Strean, H. S. Some considerations on the therapeutic neglect of fathers in child guidance. In H. S. Strean (Ed.), *New approaches in child guidance.* Metuchen, N. J.: Scarecrow Press, 1964.

Guerney, B. Filial therapy. *Journal of Consulting Psychology,* 1964, *28,* 304–310.

Gurman, A. S. Convening the family. *The American Journal of Family Therapy,* 1980, *8,* 69–72.

Haley, J. *Strategies of psychotherapy.* New York: Grune and Stratton, 1963.

Haley, J. Approaches to family therapy. In *Changing families: A family therapy reader.* New York: Grune and Stratton, 1971. (a)

Haley, J. A review of the family therapy field. In *Changing families: A family therapy reader.* New York: Grune and Stratton, 1971. (b)

Haley, J. Strategic therapy when a child is presented as the problem. *Journal of the American Academy of Child Psychiatry,* 1973, *12,* 641–659.

Harley, M. Panel report: Resistance in child analysis. *Journal of the American Psychoanalytic Association,* 1961, *9,* 548–562.

Harley, M. On some problems of technique in the analysis of early adolescents. *Psychoanalytic Study of the Child,* 1970, *25,* 99–121.

Hartmann, H. The theory of the ego. In *Essays in ego psychology.* New York: International Universities Press, 1950.

Heimann, P. On countertransference. *International Journal of PsychoAnalysis,* 1950, *31,* 81–84.

Hersen, M. Resistance to direction in behavior therapy: Some comments. *Journal of Genetic Psychology,* 1971, *118,* 121–127.

Hoffman, L. Breaking the homeostatic cycles. In P. J. Guerin (Ed.), *Family therapy.* New York: Gardner Press, 1976.

Holmes, D. J. *The adolescent in psychotherapy.* Boston: Little, Brown and Co., 1964.

Horney, K. *Self-Analysis.* New York: Norton, 1942.

Hunt, J. McV. Psychological development: Early experience. *Annual Review of Psychology,* 1979, *30,* 103–1044.

Issacharoff, A. Barriers to knowing in psychoanalysis. *Contemporary Psychoanalysis,* 1976, *12,* 407–422.

Jackson, D. D. A suggestion for the technical handling of paranoid patients. *Psychiatry,* 1963, *26,* 306–307.

Jackson, D. D. & Weakland, J. H. Conjoint family therapy: Some considerations on theory, technique and results. In *Changing families: A family therapy reader.* J. Haley, (Ed.). New York: Grune & Stratton, 1971.

Jones, J. D., & Gehman, I. H. The taboo of virginity: Resistances of male therapists and early adolescent girl patients in treatment. *Journal of the American Academy of Child Psychiatry,* 1971, *1,* 351–357.

Jouraird, S. *Self-disclosure: An experimental analysis of the transparent self.* New York: Wiley, 1971.

Kabcenell, R. J. On countertransference: The contribution of Berta Bornstein to psychoanalysis. *Psychoanalytic Study of the Child,* 1974, *29,* 27–34.

Kagan, J. *The growth of the child.* New York: W. W. Norton, 1978.

Kauffman, J. M., Kneedler, R. D., Gamache, R., Hallahan, D. P., & Ball, D. W. Effects of imitation and nonimitation in children's subsequent imitative behavior. *Journal of Genetic Psychology,* 1977, *130,* 285–293.

Kauffman, J. M., LaFleur, N. K., Hallahan, D. P., & Chanes, C. M. Imitation as a consequence for children's behavior: Two experimental studies. *Behavior Therapy,* 1975, *6,* 535–542.

Kauffman, J. M., Snell, M. E., & Hallahan, D. P. Imitating children during imitation training. *Education and Training of the Mentally Retarded,* 1976, *11,* 324–332.

Kaufman, B. N. *Son Rise.* New York: Harper & Row, 1976.

Kay, P. A survey of recent contributions on transference and transference neurosis in child analysis. In M. Kanzer (Ed.), *The unconscious today.* New York: International Universities Press, 1971.

Kernberg, O. Psychoanalytic psychotherapy with borderline adolescents. In S. C. Feinstein and P. L. Giovacchini (Eds.), *Adolescent psychiatry* (Vol. 7). Chicago: University of Chicago Press, 1979.

Kesten, J. Learning for spite. *Psychoanalysis,* 1955, 4, 63–67.

Kestenberg, J. S. Mother types encountered in child guidance clinics. *American Journal Orthopsychiatry,* 1941, *11,* 474–484.

Kestenberg, J. S. How children remember and parents forget. *International Journal of Psychoanalytic Psychotherapy,* 1972, *1,* 103–123.

King, C. H. Counter-transference and counter-experience in the treatment of violence prone youth. *American Journal of Orthopsychiatry,* 1976, 46, 43–52.

Klauber, J. The psychoanalyst as a person. *British Journal of Medical Psychology,* 1968, *41,* 315–322.

Klein, M. H., Dittman, A. T., Parloff, M. B., & Gill, M. M. Behavior therapy: Observations and reflections. *Journal of Consulting and Clinical Psychology,* 1969, *33,* 259–266.

Klumpner, G. H. A review of Freud's writings on adolescents. In S. C. Feinstein & P. L. Giovacchini (Eds.), *Adolescent psychiatry* (Vol. VI). Chicago: University of Chicago Press, 1978.

Kohrman, R., Fineberg, H. H., Gelman, R. L., & Weiss, S. Technique of child analysis: Problems of countertransference. *International Journal of PsychoAnalysis,* 1971, *52,* 487–497.

Kohut, H. *The Analysis of the self.* New York: International Universities Press, 1971.

Kohut, H. *The restoration of the self.* New York: International Universities Press, 1977.

Kramer, S., & Byerly, L. J. Technique of psychoanalysis of the latency child. In J. Glenn (Ed.), *Child analysis and therapy.* New York: Jason Aronson, 1978.

Kritzberg, N. Structured therapeutic game method of child analytic psychotherapy: dynamic game-play therapy with children. Hicksville: Exposition Press, 1975.

Kut Rosenfeld, S., & Sprince, M. P. Some thoughts on the technical handling of borderline children. *Psychoanalytic Study of the Child,* 1965, *20,* 495–517.

Lampl-de-Grott, J. On the obstacles standing in the way of psychoanalytic cure. *Psychoanalytic Study of the Child,* 1967, *22,* 20–35.

Langs, R. *The bipersonal field.* New York: Jason Aronson, 1976. (a)

Langs, R. *The therapist interaction* (Vol. II). New York: Jason Aronson, 1976. (b)

Langs, R. *Interactions: The realm of transference and countertransference.* New York: Jason Aronson, 1980.

Langs, R. Resistances and interventions. New York: Jason Aronson, 1981.

Langs, R. J. The patient's unconscious perception of the therapist's errors. In P. L. Giovacchini (Ed.), *Tactics and techniques in psychoanalytic therapy, Vol. II. Countertransference.* New York: Jason Aronson, 1975.

Lebovici, S. Countertransference in child analysis. *Psyche,* 1951, *11,* 680–687.

Lebovici, S., Dratkine, R., Favreau, J. A., & Laquet-Parat, P. The psychoanalysis of children. In S. Nacht (Ed.), *Psychoanalysis of today.* New York: Grune and Stratton, 1970. (a)

Lebovici, S., Dratkine, R., & Kestemberg, E. Bilan de dix ans de practique chez l'enfant et l'adolescent. *Bulletin de Psychologie,* 1970, *23,* 839–888. (b)

Levant, R. F. A classification of the field of family therapy. *American Journal of Family Therapy.* 1980, *8,* 3–17.

Levy, D. Maternal overprotection *Psychiatry,* 1939, 2, 99–128.

Levy, K. Simultaneous analysis of a mother and her adolescent daughter. *Psychoanalytic Study of the Child,* 1960, *15,* 378–391.

Lewis, M. & Brooks-Gunn, J. *Social cognition and the acquisition of self.* New York: Plenum Press, 1979.

Lidz, T., Fleck, S. and Cornelison, A. R. *Schizophrenia and the family.* New York: International Universities Press, 1965.

Lilleskov, R. K. Transference and transference neurosis in child analysis. In M. Kanzer (Ed.), *The unconscious today.* New York: International Universities Press, 1971.

Lindner, R. *The Fifty minute hour: A collection of true psychoanalytic tales.* New York: Rinehart, 1955.

Little, M. Countertransference and the patient's response to it. *International Journal of PsychoAnalysis,* 1951, *32,* 32–40.

Love, S., & Mayer, H. Going along with defenses in resistive families. *Social Casework, 40,* 1959, 130–135.

MacCorquodale, K., & Meehl, P. E. Hypothetical constructs and intervening variables. *Psychological Review,* 1948, *55,* 95–107.

Maenchen, A. On the technique of child analysis in relation to stages of development. *Psychoanalytic Study of the Child,* 1970, *25,* 175–208.

Marcus, I. M. Countertransference and the psychoanalytic process in children and adults. *Psychoanalytic Study of the Child,* 1980, *35,* 285–298.

Margolis, B. *Joining.* Unpublished manuscript, 1981.

Marohn, R. C. The "juvenile imposter": Some thoughts on narcissism and the delinquent. In S. C. Feinstein and P. L. Giovacchini (Eds.), *Adolescent psychiatry* (Vol. V). New York: Aronson, 1977.

Marshall, R. J. Variation on self-attitudes and attitudes toward others as a function of peer group appraisals. Doctoral dissertation, University of Buffalo, 1958.

Marshall, R. J. The treatment of resistance of children and adolescents to psychotherapy. *Psychotherapy: Research and Practice,* 1972, *9,* 143–148.

Marshall, R. J. Meeting the resistances of delinquents. *The Psychoanalytic Review,* 1974, *61,* 295–304.

Marshall, R. J. "Joining techniques" in the treatment of resistant children and adolescents. *American Journal of Psychotherapy,* 1976, *30,* 73–84.

Marshall, R. J. The rise and fall of a milieu therapy program. *Residential and Community Child Care Administration,* 1978, *1,* 265–276.

Marshall, R. J. Antisocial youth. In J. D. Noshpitz (Ed.), *Basic handbook of child psychiatry* (Vol. III). New York: Basic Books, 1979. (a)

Marshall, R. J. Countertransference in the psychotherapy of children and adolescence. In L. Epstein and A. H. Feiner (Eds.), *Countertransference: The therapist's contribution to treatment.* New York: Aronson, 1979. (b)

Marshall, S. Filial therapy: The therapy of a mother–child symbiosis. Unpublished manuscript, 1978.

Masterson, J. F. *Treatment of the borderline adolescent: A developmental approach.* New York: Wiley-Interscience, 1972.

Meadow, P. W. A research method for investigating the effectiveness of psychoanalytic techniques. *Psychoanalytic Review,* 1974, *61,* 79–94.

Menninger, K. *Theory of psychoanalytic technique.* New York: Basic Books, 1958.

Meltzoff, A. N. and Moore, M. K. Imitation of facial and manual gestures by human neonates. *Science* 1977, 198, 75–78.

Miller, N. E. Liberalizations of basic S–R concepts: Extensions to conflict behavior, motivation and social learning in psychology. In S. Koch (Ed.), *A study of a science* (Study I, Vol. 2). New York: McGraw–Hill, 1959.

Miller, N. E. Some animal experiments pertinent to the problem of combining psychotherapy with drug therapy. *Comprehensive Psychiatry,* 1966, *1,* 1–12.

Moustakas, C. E. *Children in play therapy.* New York: McGraw–Hill, 1953.

Nelson, M. C. *Roles and paradigms in psychotherapy.* New York: Grune & Stratton, 1968.

Neubauer, P. The nonengaging child. In E. J. Anthony and D. C. Gilpin (Eds.), *The three clinical faces of childhood.* New York: Spectrum, 1976.

Novick, J. Negative therapeutic motivation and negative therapeutic alliance. *Psychoanalytic Study of the Child,* 1980, *35,* 299–320.

Ogden, T. H. On projective identification. *International Journal of Psychoanalysis,* 1979, *60,* 357–373.

Orbach, J., Traub, A. C., & Olson, R. Psychophysical studies of body-image: II Normative data on the adjustable body-distorting mirror. *Archives of General Psychiatry,* 1966, 14, 41–47.

Oremland, J. D. Transference cure and flight into health. *International Journal of Psychoanalytic Psychotherapy,* 1972, *1,* 61–75.

Palazzoli, M. S., Boscolo, L., Lecchin, G., & Prata, G. *Paradox and counterparadox: A new model in the therapy of the family in schizophrenic transaction.* New York: Aronson, 1978.

Paul, G. L. *Insight vs. desensitization in psychotherapy: An experiment in anxiety reduction.* Stanford, Calif: Stanford University Press, 1966.

Pearson, G. H. J. (Ed.). *A handbook of child psychoanalysis.* New York: Basic Books, 1968.

Pestalozzi, J. H. *Leonard and Gertrude.* New York: Gordon Press 1976.

Piaget, J. *Play, dreams and imitation in childhood.* New York: Norton, 1962.

Piaget, J. *The mechanisms of perception.* New York: Basic Books, 1969.

Pichon-Riviére, E. Quelques considerations sur le transfert et le contre transfert dans la psychanalyse d'enfants. *Revue Française de Psychanalyse,* 1952, *16,* 231–253.

Proctor, J. T. Countertransference phenomena in the treatment of severe character disorders in children and adolescents. In L. Jessner and E. Davenstedt (Eds.), *Dynamic psychopathology in childhood.* New York: Grune & Stratton, 1959.

Racker, H. Meanings and uses of countertransference. *Psychoanalytic Quarterly,* 1957, *26,* 303–357.

Rank, Otto. *Will therapy and truth in reality.* New York: Alfred Knopf, 1945.

Reich, A. On countertransference. *International Journal of PsychoAnalysis,* 1951, *33,* 25–31.

Reich, A. Further remarks on countertransference. *International Journal of PsychoAnalysis,* 1960, *41,* 389–395.

Reich, W. *Character analysis,* 3rd Ed. New York: Orgone Institute Press, 1949.

Rheingold, J. C. *The mother, anxiety, and death.* Boston: Little, Brown and Company, 1967.

Rhoads, J. M., & Feather, B. W. Transference and resistance observed in behavior therapy. *British Journal of Medical Psychology,* 1972, *45,* 99–103.

Rinsley, D. B. *Treatment of the severely disturbed adolescent.* New York: Jason Aronson, 1980.

Ritvo, S. The psychoanalytic process in childhood. *Psychoanalytic Study of the Child,* 1978, *33,* 295–305.

Roberts, M. C. The effects on the model of being imitiated: A review and critique of the literature. *JSAS Catalog of Selected Documents in Psychology,* 1979, *9,* 1–19.

Rogers, C. *On becoming a person: A therapist's view of psychotherapy.* Boston: Houghton–Mifflin, 1961.

Rosenthal, L. The origins and development of the concept of resistance in analytic group psychotherapy. Doctoral dissertation, Heed University, 1978.

Rubenstein, B. O., & Levitt, M. Some observations regarding the role of fathers in child psychotherapy. *Bulletin of the Menninger Clinic,* 1957, *21,* 16–27.

Sandler, J. Countertransference and role-responsiveness. *International Review of PsychoAnalysis,* 1976, *3,* 43–47.

Sandler, J., Dare, C., & Holder, A. *The Patient and analyst: The basis of the psychoanalytic process.* New York: International Universities Press, 1973.

Sandler, J., Kennedy, H., & Tyson, R. L. Discussions on transference. *Psychoanalytic Study of the Child,* 1975, *30,* 409–411.

Sanders, W. B. *Juvenile offenders for a thousand years.* Durham: University of North Carolina Press, 1970.

Sarnoff, C. *Latency.* New York: Jason Aronson, 1976.

Satir, V., *Conjoint family therapy.* Palo Alto: Science & Behavior Books.

Schafer, R. The idea of resistance. *International Journal of PsychoAnalysis,* 1973, *54,* 259–285.

Scharfman, M. A. Transference and the transference neurosis in child analysis. In J. Glenn (Ed.), *Child analysis and therapy.* New York: Jason Aronson, 1978.

Searles, H. F. The patient as therapist to his analyst. In P. L. Giovacchini (Ed.), *Tactics and techniques in psychoanalytic therapy, Vol. II, countertransference.* New York: Jason Aronson, Inc., 1975.

Shengold, L. The metaphor of the mirror. *Journal of the American Psychoanalytic Association,* 1974, *22,* 97–115.

Shermo, S. F., Paynter, J., & Szurek, S. A. Problems of staff interaction with spontaneous group formations in a children's psychiatric ward. *American Journal of Orthopsychiatry,* 1949, *19,* 599–611.

Singer, E. *Key concepts in psychotherapy.* New York: Random House, 1965.

Slavson, S. R. *Child psychotherapy.* New York: Columbia University Press, 1952.

Slavson, S. R. Eclecticism versus sectarianism in group psychotherapy. *International Journal of Group Psychotherapy,* 1970, 20, 3–13.

Sonne, J. C., Speck, R. V., & Jungreis, J. E. The absent-member maneuver as a resistance in family therapy of schizophrenics. *Family Process,* 1962, *1,* 44–62.

Sperling, M. Analytic first aid in school phobia. *Psychoanalytic Quarterly,* 1961, 30, 504–518.

Spitz, R. A. Countertransference: Comments on its varying role in the analytic situation. *Journal of the American Psychoanalytic Association,* 1956, *4,* 256–265.

Spitz, R. A. *No and yes: On the genesis of human communication.* New York: International Universities Press, 1957.

Spitz, R. A. *The first year of life.* New York: International Universities Press, 1965.

Spotnitz, H. *Modern psychoanalysis of the schizophrenic patient.* New York: Grune & Stratton, 1969.

Spotnitz, H. Observations on child analysis. *Modern Psychoanalysis,* 1976, *1,* 33–42. (a)

Spotnitz, H. *The psychotherapy of preoedipal conditions.* New York: Aronson, 1976. (b)

Spotnitz, H., Nagelberg, L., & Feldman, Y. Ego reinforcement. In H. Spotnitz, *Psychotherapy of preoedipal conditions.* New York: Aronson, 1976.

Sprince, M. The development of a preoedipal partnership between an adolescent girl and her mother. *Psychoanalytic Study of the Child*, 1962, *17,* 418–450.

Stampfl, T. G. Implosive therapy. In P. Olsen (Ed.), *Emotional flooding.* New York: Human Sciences Press, 1976.

Sterba, R. F. Aggression in the rescue fantasy. *Psychoanalytic Quarterly,* 1940, 9, 505–508.

Stierlin, H. Countertransference in family therapy with adolescents. In

M. Sugar (Ed.), *The adolescent in group and family therapy.* New York: Brunner/Mazel, 1975.

Stolorow, R. D. Psychoanalytic reflections on client-centered therapy in the light of modern conceptions of narcissism. *Psychotherapy: Theory, Research and Practice,* 1976, *13,* 26–29.

Stolorow, R. D., & Lachmann, F. M. *Psychoanalysis of developmental arrests: Theory and treatment.* New York: International Universities Press, 1980.

Stone, L. The psychoanalytic situation and transference: Postscript to an earlier communication. *Journal of the American Psychological Association*, 1967, *15,* 3–58.

Strean, H. S. Paradigmatic interventions in seemingly difficult therapeutic situations. In M. C. Nelson, B. Nelson, M. H. Sherman, & H. S. Strean (Eds.), *Roles and paradigms in psychotherapy.* New York: Grune & Stratton, 1968.

Strean, H. S. (Ed.). *New approaches in child guidance.* Metuchen, N. J.: Scarecrow Press, 1970.

Szurek, S. A. Problems around psychotherapy with children. *Journal of Pediatrics,* 1950, *37,* 671–678.

Taft, J. *The dyanmics of therapy in a controlled relationship.* New York: Dover Publications, Inc., 1962.

Tauber, E. Exploring the therapeutic use of contertransference data. *Psychiatry,* 1954, *17,* 331–336.

Tower, L. E. Countertransference. *Journal of the American Psychoanalytic Association,* 1956, *4,* 224–255.

Truax, C. B., & Carkhuff, R. R. *Toward effective counseling and psychotherapy: Training and practice.* Chicago: Aldine, 1967.

Tylum, I. Narcissistic transference and countertransference in adolescent treatment. *Psychoanalytic Study of the Child,* 1978, *33,* 279–292.

Van Dam, H. Panel: Problems of transference in child analysis. *Journal of the American Psychoanalytic Association,* 1966, *14,* 528–537.

Van Riper, C. *Speech correction.* (5th Ed.) Englewood Cliffs, N.J.: Prentice-Hall, 1972.

Wachtel, P. L. *Psychoanalysis and behavior therapy.* New York: Basic Books, 1973.

Waters, D. B. Family therapy as a defense. *Journal of the American Academy of Child Psychiatry,* 1976, *15,* 464–474.

Watzlawick, P. *The language of change.* New York: Basic Books, 1978.

Watzlawick, P., Beavin, J. H., & Jackson, D. D. *Pragmatics of human communication.* New York: W. W. Norton, 1967.

Weakland, J. Communication theory and clinical change. In P. J. Guerin, Jr. (Ed.), *Family therapy.* New York: Gardner Press, 1976.

Webster's Third New International Dictionary. Chicago: Encyclopaedia Britannica, Inc., 1966.

Weil, A. P. Ego strengthening prior to analysis. *Psychoanalytic Study of the Child,* 1973, *28,* 287–301.

Weinberg, N. H., & Zaslove, M. "Resistance" to systematic desensitization of phobias. *Journal of Clinical Psychology,* 1963, *19,* 179–181.

Weiss, S., Fineberg, H. H. Gelman, R. L. & Korman, R. Techniques of child analysis. *Journal American Academy of Child Psychiatry.* 1968, 7, 639–662.

Welsh, R. S. The use of stimulus satiation in the elimination of juvenile fire-setting behavior. In A. M. Graziano (Ed.), *Behavior therapy with children.* Chicago: Aldine, 1971.

Whitaker, C. A., Felder, R. E., Malone, T. P., & Warkenton, J. First stage techniques in the experiential psychotherapy of chronic schizophrenic patients. In J. H. Masserman (Ed.), *Current psychiatric therapies* (Vol. 2). New York: Grune & Stratton, 1962.

Whitaker, C. A., Felder, R. E., & Warkenton, J. Countertransference in the family treatment of schizophrenia. In I. Boszormeny & J. L. Framo (Eds.), *Intensive family therapy: Theoretical and practical aspects.* New York: Harper and Row, 1965.

Winnicott, D. W. *Collected papers.* London: Tavistock Publications, 1958.

Winnicott, D. W. *Playing and reality.* New York: Basic Books, 1971.

Wolberg, A. R. *The Borderline patient.* New York: International Medical Book Corp., 1973.

Wolberg, L. R. *The technique of psychotherapy.* New York: Grune & Stratton, 1977.

Wolman, B. B. (Ed.). *Success and failure in psychoanalysis and psychotherapy.* New York: Macmillan, 1972.

Wolstein, B. Freedom to experience. New York: Grune & Stratton, 1964.

Wylie, R. C. The self-concept: A critical survey of pertinent research literature. Lincoln: University of Nebraska Press, 1961.

Wylie, R. C. The self-concept: Theory and research in selected topics. Lincoln: University of Nebraska Press, 1979.

NAME INDEX

SUBJECT INDEX